DATE DUE			

SOME LETTERS OF
William Vaughn Moody

William Vaughn Moody

1869–1910

SOME LETTERS

OF

William Vaughn Moody

EDITED WITH AN INTRODUCTION

BY

DANIEL GREGORY MASON

AMS PRESS
NEW YORK

Reprinted from the edition of 1913, Boston and New York
First AMS EDITION published 1969
Manufactured in the United States of America

Library of Congress Catalogue Card Number: 76-94471

AMS PRESS, INC.
NEW YORK, N. Y. 10003

INTRODUCTION

"HE liberates the imagination with his prose," wrote one of Moody's friends when the project of collecting some of the letters was being discussed, "as effectively as he does with his poetry. And then besides there is the luminous personality which emerges from every folded sheet, looking out with large veiled eyes." The comment happily describes the double interest of these letters. They are, first of all, literature, and may be read, by those who know nothing of the personality of their author, for their purely literary charm, their power to "liberate the imagination." They carry, like his poetry, for such a reader, their own rich gifts of delight; they are as magnanimously conceived, as hauntingly phrased, as eloquently and ingeniously clothed in metaphor, even more mischievously touched with humor. Moody's poetry is destined, surely, to a high, if not to the supreme, place in the American poetry of his generation. His letters, it seems to me, are worthy to stand beside it; and there, so far as their purely literary quality is concerned, they may be left without further comment.

But like all good letters they are not only literature but self-revelation; and the clear vision of this more individual element may be helped not only by the large illumination shed upon them from the poetry, but by the countless casual side-lights that only per-

INTRODUCTION

sonal acquaintance can note and interpret. The two
or three essential qualities of Moody's mind were
singularly persistent and ubiquitous, and like the few
geologic strata that may underlie the most varied
landscape, cropped out in his careless talk as unmis-
takably as in his poems or letters. His spiritual earn-
estness, for example, made him as indifferent to the
merely conventional aspects of life as he was passion-
ately curious about its essential structure. In his
poetry he avoided superficial detail, to penetrate at
once to essences. In his letters he often exasperatingly
withheld the petty facts of which most correspondence
consists, but was always frank and full in the reve-
lation of mood. Similarly in everyday intercourse he
combined intellectual candor and personal reserve in a
way that many found bewildering. For his friends the
paradox was symbolised in his eyes. In their liquidness
and transparence, in their steadfastness and quietude,
they seemed to open up quite fearlessly a way to his
deepest thoughts. Beautiful serene eyes they were,
telling all that mattered but ignoring the trivial and
the irrelevant: it was as if he had both the honesty
and the shyness of a child. This is perhaps what
his friend means when he speaks of his personality
"emerging from every folded sheet, with large veiled
eyes."

Akin to the serenity of his gaze, and like it a little
embarrassing on first acquaintance but endlessly re-
freshing to riper friendship, was his constitutional
taciturnity. It used to be said of him in college that

INTRODUCTION

"It took Moody a pipeful to make a remark"—and the discerning added that it was worth while to wait. When I first met him, in the spring of 1894, during his instructorship in the English Department at Harvard, his manner was shy and somewhat self-consciously awkward, so that we undergraduates of a complacent local clique found it easy to dismiss him as "Western." An odd blend of floridity and negligence about him offended those whose ideal of manliness was a correct dandyism. And in his physical being there was indeed a sort of rough homeliness that made the epithet to a certain extent descriptive. But it did not take long to pass that stage, to find that he had also the freshness and magnanimity of the West, and that he saw things under wider horizons than those of the Cambridge tea-tables. Above all, one discovered the richness of his silences. He had a way of slightly knitting his brows, as if taking, from under half-closed lids, a bird's-eye view of the broadest possible stretch of his subject, while he communed with his pipe, frequently pressing down the tobacco with a forefinger long inured to that service, and finally producing a brief comment, usually metaphorical and often madly exaggerative, that liberated the mind more than floods of ordinary talk. It was as if, instead of dissipating the thought supply as most talkers do, churning it up into a froth that gives only an illusion of increased substance, he was engaged in a quiet husbanding of truth, whereby it rose to higher levels in the reservoir. He gave one always a sense of increased insight, of renewed confidence, of a deeper and truer conspectus of things than that of everyday observation.

The liberating effect of his talk must have been due in no small degree to its vividly figurative quality. No matter to what extent one might have been led to expect this by the luxuriance of figure characteristic of his poetry, one could not but be struck afresh on each occasion, by the surprising variety, the ingenious complexity, and often the droll incongruity, of the metaphors that he would constantly strike out in the heat of conversation, mould with loving care for a moment, and then toss aside. The letters, too, it will be found, owe much of their individuality of flavor to a use of figure at once whimsical and persistently logical. Who but Moody would have thought of comparing himself to a bicycle in such elaborate detail as this: "Good fun, but rather hard on one's tire. I hasten to assure you that I am as yet unpunctured, though much worn at the rim, and rapidly losing resiliency by leakage. I relinquish the figure with reluctance." On another occasion, trying to solace a friend incapacitated for work, he lets himself be beguiled into some charming variations on the old theme, "The dark cellar ripens the wine." "And meanwhile," he says, "after one's eyes get used to the dirty light, and one's feet to the mildew, a cellar has its compensations. I have found beetles of the most interesting proclivities, mice altogether comradely and persuadable, and forgotten potatoes that sprouted toward the crack of sunshine with a wan maiden grace not seen above." But the

INTRODUCTION

most irresistible instance, in all the letters, of this peculiarly Moody-esque pursuit, with meticulous logic, of a more or less absurd metaphor, occurs in a letter to Mrs. Toy in which he hits off once for all that contrast between East and West which was always haunting him. "I am eager," he writes, "for the queer inimitable charm of Cambridge, for that atmosphere of mind at once so impersonal and so warm, for that neatness and decency of you children, who have been washed and dressed and sent to play on the front lawn of time by old auntie Ding-an-sich, while we hoodlums contend with the goat for tomato cans in the alley. I have a fair line of the same to lay before your eyes when I am admitted inside the aristocratic front gate: some of them will make a fine effect in a ring around your geranium bed."

Conceive this vigorous image-making faculty irresponsibly applied to the thousand and one subjects of casual talk; conceive it stimulated by the enthusiasm of youthful comradeships, and invited by the endless leisure of vagrant country walks in spring, or of long winter evenings spent toasting before an open-grate fire, in an atmosphere of tobacco smoke and hot rum toddy; conceive it returning upon itself at will, and constructing day by day a special cosmogony and vocabulary of its own. One such winter evening I shall never forget, when in the small hours the talk grew youthfully philosophic, and Moody, his ever ruddy face flushed with the excitement of improvisation, leaning out from swirls of smoke and emphasizing his points with outstretched pipe, drew a picture of man in the universe as a frog in a well, condemned always to darkness, destined never to know what was in the world above. I dare say it was only warmed-over Kantianism; certainly the toddy contributed much to its impressiveness; but when the rich cadences of his voice died away it was to a solemn silence, with the two youthful philosophers thoroughly awed at their own imaginings.

Something of the same solemnity that invests that image of the frog in the well hangs about certain other conceptions that acquired for us, chiefly from Moody's eloquence, a largely representative value. "It," for example, referred to in the letters, transcends the explanation it seems to require, because it both denotes something so indefinable, and connotes something so incommunicable. "It" is everything, taken together, that may be the object of a youthful idealist's devotion; it is the sum total of all that is beautiful and worthy of loyalty in the world; it is what it is happiness to remember, wretchedness to forget. A "diastole," also mentioned in the letters, is a mood in which, so to speak, the spiritual circulation is good (the figure is, of course, drawn from the physiology of the heart); it is a mood of vitality, of realization, of fulfilment. Such moods we made it a point of honor, as well as a privilege, to celebrate by communication. Systoles we may also have experienced, but usually we had the courage not to talk about them. The most curious term of all, naming a type of humanity rather than a general idea, was

INTRODUCTION

"Pritchard" — originally the name of a young working-man we met one evening during one of our long aimless walks. In some occult way he typified for us Philistinism — all the dull, prosaic world which was our enemy. In some still more occult way (though possibly cocktails had something to do with it) he mystically blossomed into one of the elect. From that time forth, "Pritchard" was for us the divinity in the average man.

Crudely youthful as were some of these notions and formulations, they played a genuine part in Moody's development, and reverberations of them may be caught by the attentive ear throughout his poems and letters. They were at any rate generous, and sprang from a fine idealistic enthusiasm. Moreover, they illustrate, in their persistent tendency to take on figurative form, what one comes finally to consider the fundamental quality of his mind. Metaphor was his natural mode of expression. It occurred to him as spontaneously for a capricious snap-shot at everyday life as for the more deliberate description in a letter or for the noble setting-forth of his poetic dramas. Its manifestations in casual talk had one element of charm peculiarly their own. One does not get, alas, in the poetry, or even in the letters, the comment of personal gesture and inflection on these crowding figments of his fancy: the gathering amusement in his eyes as he elaborated some conceit; the portentous seriousness with which he brought forth his exaggerations or absurdities; the final bursting shout of laughter, when the dam gave way, that shook his whole frame with its physical gusto.

The distinctive trait of his mind was thus, I have always thought, rather its imaginative power than its purely intellectual scope or subtlety: he was far more poet than philosopher. There is in his books, to be sure, even though it be obscured sometimes, especially in the prose plays, by touches of sentimentalism, a wisdom both noble and broad; in daily intercourse one loved the sweetness and sanity of his mind quite as much as one admired its bold constructiveness; and his imagination itself, however untrammeled, owed much of its vigor to a kind of tenacious consecutiveness akin to logic. Nevertheless must one insist that he characteristically saw the world not from the detached point of view of philosophy, and under its cold, even illumination, but rather as a glowing focus where the rays of passionate sympathetic interest for the moment converged, brilliantly relieved against semi-obscurity. He leaned always toward the extremes of statement in which such a vision, with its sharp chiaroscuro, naturally expresses itself. He was too eager in the vivid presentment of what he had felt intensely to linger over peddling accuracies of qualification. He seized upon his subject, isolated and magnified it. Many amusing instances of his exaggeration may be found in the letters. "There are three hundred and twenty-three hand-organs and ninety-seven pianos on our block," he writes from his New York lodgings in 1900, "and every hour thirty-five thousand drays

INTRODUCTION

loaded with sheet-iron pass the house. Irving Place, you know, is a quiet old-fashioned neighborhood, so we are justly proud of these slight evidences of animation." From Chicago he sends the plaint, during one of his periods of teaching: "I counted my vocabulary last night, and discovered it to consist of ninety-three words. You shall have them all, if you will promise not to be reckless with them." Such passages as these help us to understand the over-luxuriance of his youthful poetic style. If we consider, furthermore, that his native tendency to extravagance was fostered, almost from the first, by an acquired rhetorical virtuosity the exercise of which must have been highly exciting, we shall be able to account for the turgidity of much of his early verse.

But if both temperament and technical skill thus inclined him rather toward romantic luxuriance than toward classic chastity, only the more remarkable becomes the tireless discipline by which he trained himself to achieve the sobriety and distinction of such later pieces as, say, the lyrics in "The Fire-Bringer." We are reminded of Verdi's progress from "Il Trovatore" to "Otello," or Wagner's from "Rienzi" to "Die Meistersinger," by a poet who begins with rococo effects like

> "Yet her shy devious lambent soul
> With my slow soul should walk," [1]

and ends with such noble simplicities as

[1] See first draft of "Wilding Flower," page 58.

INTRODUCTION

"Of wounds and sore defeat
I made my battle stay;
Wingèd sandals for my feet
I wove of my delay;
Of weariness and fear
I made my shouting spear;
Of loss, and doubt, and dread,
And swift oncoming doom,
I made a helmet for my head
And a floating plume." [1]

No one not endowed by nature with a vivid imagination and an eagerly sympathetic spirit could have written lines like these; but furthermore, no one thus endowed could have written them, had he not long schooled himself in the subtle arts of moderation, just emphasis, and suggestion. I hardly know which the more to admire in Moody as a poet, the native richness of his mind, or the patient art by which he learned to draw from it so pure a harmony.

The reader may perhaps welcome, for the insight they give into both qualities, a few more examples of his early work than he decided to include in the "Poems" of 1901. What he rejected then, as not representative of his artistry at its best, we may now find well worth study, as revealing something of the processes by which it was attained, especially when we can examine the piece in the light of his own comment, as in the case of "Wilding Flower." "Heart's Wild-Flower," as he renamed the revised form of it printed

[1] "The Fire-Bringer," Act I.

xiv

in the "Poems," is one of his loveliest lyrics. It succeeds in saying what he considered to be "a thing which constitutes much of the poetry of a young man's life," and in saying it not more eloquently than simply, with much of exquisite music, and no jarring notes. With this version well in mind, turn to the first draft, sent with the letter of May 16, 1896,[1] and examine it in some detail. First of all may be noted so apparently trivial a matter as the way of printing the stanza: six short verses in the earlier form, three long ones in the later. The short verses break the free sweep of the rhythm. In many places the difference may be negligible, but at the end of the next to the last stanza, for example, the wondrous charm of the rhythm is much enhanced by printing all in one line

"Awes, adorations, songs of ruth, hesitancies, and tears."

Secondly, the author has ruthlessly deleted stanzas II–VIII of the original version — more than half of the entire poem. So heroic an amputation was necessitated chiefly by the obscurity of the suspended construction in stanzas IV–VI, which he admitted only after considerable argument, and reluctantly, as will be seen from the letter of June 23. Indeed, as in most revisions, there was here a loss as well as a gain; for he was quite right in pointing out the effect of "breathlessness and holding aloof" secured by the suspension, and in comparing its constructive value to that of an organ point in music. The omission of stanza III also sacrifices the

[1] Page 56.

XV

delicate preparation it made for the final stanza. But
sacrifices are not sacrifices unless they cost something,
and skillful revision consists precisely in this wise
balancing of complex accounts. It was worth while at
almost any price to get rid of the "flushed adventurous violins," "the tower noon-precipiced," and the
"aching oboe throat that twins Night's moonward
melodist," which are the youthful Moody at his
worst.

In the third place, the substitutions made in the
retained stanzas are all noteworthy, most of them
because they tend toward simplicity. Such, for instance, are "spirit fire" for "lilac fire," "crown of
tears and flame" for "carcanet of flame," "autumn
woe" for "subtle woe," "a little gift" for "a mystic
gift," and the poignant "shy, shy wilding flowers" for
the rather literary "lovesome wilding flowers." Most
interesting of all, however, are the alterations in the
third stanza of the present version, as not merely
verbal but affecting the conception itself, toning it
down from the extreme and acrid terms into which
Moody's instinct for potent expression had led him,
into much juster, tenderer ones.

> "Not such a sign as women wear
> Who bow beneath the shame
> Of marriage insolence, and bear
> A housewife's faded name" —

which exaggerates the contrast and repels us by its
harshness, becomes —

INTRODUCTION

"Not such a sign as women wear who make their foreheads
     tame
With life's long tolerance, and bear love's sweetest, humblest
     name."

Here the rhetorical antithesis remains unimpaired,
and there is a marked gain in spiritual propriety, and
consequently in artistic dignity.

Finally it is well to note, after we have made all
possible criticism of this first draft on the scores of
obscurity of construction, turgidity of thought, or
intemperance of language, that these are after all the
faults of excess rather than of defect, and that in spite
of them, and in some degree even because of them, the
mind at work here shows itself to be thoroughly alive.
If it has the crudity, it has also the teeming vitality of
youth. Its exuberance is infinitely to be preferred to the
pallid correctness of academicism. Its mistakes are
those of a generous, independent nature daring enough
to attempt something new, and its failures are of the
inspiring kind that in all artistic paths pave the way to
future successes. One is glad to think that even in his
moments of discouragement he had the pioneer's sus-
taining sense of adventure and discovery, as when he
writes: "I think — pardon the egotism of the utterance
(you would if you knew what tears of failure have gone
to water the obstreperous little plant) — I think you
are not tolerant enough of the instinct for conquest in
language, the attempt to push out its boundaries, to
win for it continually some new swiftness, some rare
compression, to distil from it a more opaline drop.

Is n't it possible, too, to be pedantic in the demand for simplicity? It's a cry which, if I notice aright, nature has a jaunty way of disregarding. Command a rosebush in the stress of June to purge itself; coerce a convolvulus out of the paths of catachresis. Amen!"

In this endeavor, thus early put before himself as a conscious ideal, to win for language "some new swiftness, some rare compression," Moody found, as time went on, not only an unfailing interest, but an object worthy his most tireless devotion, his most unswerving loyalty: he had the passion of the old alchemists for the distillation of that "more opaline drop." Impatient as he might be of the drudgery of teaching or hackwriting, in his poetic work no labor could dismay him. He loved to take pains. I especially remember the trick he had, in his rough drafts, of making endless substitutions of words, choosing first one and then another, striking out each in turn and surmounting it with the next, until some of his lines looked like the pediments of ruined temples, with columns of words rising at irregular intervals to unequal heights. To find him in his studio on a working morning (if one had the temerity), in a cloud of tobacco smoke, threading a labyrinth of emendations, surrounded by the carnage of previous encounters — burnt matches, scattered ashes, and discarded sheets — was to conceive a new respect for an art which could so completely conceal itself. His production was necessarily slow. The "Masque of Judgment," for example, was begun in the summer of 1897, written out in fragmentary shape a year later

INTRODUCTION

during the holiday in Italy, and elaborated in London in the spring of 1899 to twice its previous proportions. "There are," he mentions in December of that year, "counting rewriting and further development here and there, about five hundred lines to be added." It was finally completed in Boston early in 1900. "The Faith-Healer," which was not finished until the last year of his life, 1910, was begun, as the letters show, fifteen years before, in December, 1895.

Some sense of the devotion and the deliberateness with which he wrote his poetry is necessary to an understanding of his loathing for what he calls in one of his early Chicago letters "the crowd of spiteful assiduous nothings that keep me from It." Although he recognized with his usual fair-mindedness that he must pay his way by teaching or some similar form of "useful" work, and punctilious as he was in the discharge of these duties, he could not but resent their intrusion on time that he needed for work of infinitely greater intrinsic value. And they not only absorbed his time — they dulled his mental edge, and when long continued robbed him of "the spirit of selection, the zest of appropriation" which is the life of an artist. Consequently no note is more recurrent in the first letters from Chicago than that of a discontent with his new surroundings which was doubtless only partly due to the specific quality of the place, and is chiefly to be attributed to the distastefulness of his pursuits there.

Indeed the comments on Chicago, though all interesting, are oddly contradictory, and suggest a ceaseless alternation of moods. The mere physical spaciousness of the Western landscape seems sometimes to have oppressed, sometimes to have excited him. "Cambridge, mellow and autumnal," he writes soon after his arrival, "begins already to loom symbolic, under the stress of this relentless prairie light and vast featureless horizon." Yet, a month later, "To be a poet," he cries, "is a much better thing than to write poetry — out here, at least, watched by these wide horizons, beckoned to by these swift streamers of victorious sunset." Both of these opposed moods are not only expressed but philosophically penetrated in the beautiful letter of February 16, 1896, about the Irish girl he met skating.

What he called the "Western heartiness and uniplexity" subjected him to similar fluctuations of feeling. "As for Chicago," he tells Mrs. Toy, "I find that it gives me days or at least hours of broad-gauge Whitmanesque enthusiasm, meagrely sprinkled over weeks of tedium." In the long run he seems to have felt the deprivations more than the advantages: "In the East . . . one had n't to go far before finding some refinement of feeling, some delicate arabesque of convention, to help make up for the lack of liberty. Out here there is even less liberty (because less thought) and there is nothing — or next to nothing — to compensate." He describes in a memorable sentence of the same letter the deadly effect of such monotony on his eagerly adventurous mind — "that awful hush settling down on everything, as if Tὸ Πᾶν had suddenly discovered himself to be stuffed with sawdust."

The truth is, Moody was not made to wear contentedly, anywhere, the academic harness and blinders: he was too full of the untamable wildness of the creative mind which he has expressed so incomparably in his "Road-Hymn for the Start."

"Dear shall be the banquet table where their singing spirits press;
Dearer be our sacred hunger, and our pilgrim loneliness."

No one so insatiably curious about life as he was, so ardent to learn, could give himself with patience to teaching. How many times must he have felt that impulse he confesses to "trundle his little instructorial droning-gear into Lake Michigan, and step out west or south on the Open Road, a free man by the grace of God, and a tramp by Rachel's intercession"! How dead and buried must he have seemed to himself when he computed in January, 1898, "April is only eighty-eight lectures, forty committee meetings, and several thousand themes away"! And how archly, a little later, as the months nevertheless elapse, does he paraphrase Wordsworth: "My heart leaps up when I behold a calendar on the sly"! When the vacations do at last arrive, and he is free once more to take up his own work, it is exciting to read of his joy. "I can feel the holy influences that wait on him who loafs beginning to purge me and urge me, though I tremble to say so for fear of frightening back their shy inquiring tentacles." "The summer I am bound to have though the Heavens fall, or rather because they are not going to fall but remain as a fittingly modest framework for the spectacle of my felicity."

It is worth while to insist with some amplitude of detail on the disharmony between Moody's economic conditions and his spiritual needs, both because his resolution of the discord was accomplished with a tact and courage that reveal much of what is finest in his character, and more generally because this Apollo-Admetus problem is fundamental in the life of every artist, and Moody's example is therefore a widely inspiring one. His friends could never sufficiently admire the quiet self-respect with which he pursued a course midway between the extremes where so many gifted natures meet shipwreck. In the first place, he was both too honest and too shrewd to shirk his service to Admetus — that irreducible minimum of it which he had decided to be necessary. He could even, thanks to his imagination, take the point of view of the task-master, see what was reasonably to be expected of the servant, and understand the fatuity of evading it. He always fulfilled his obligations to the letter. When he was working on his "History of English Literature," for instance, at Gloucester, in May, 1900, — a month when moors and sea are at their most seductive, — he may have found it necessary, as he whimsically states, to "put on blinders, stuff his ears with wax, and strap himself to the desk"; but at least the work done in that constricted position was solid and workmanlike, as any one may see for himself.

On the other hand, he never forgot for a moment that such work was but a means to an end; he never tolerated the sentimental fallacy that faithfulness in the treadmill exempts one from the higher responsibilities of a liberal leisure; he never gave Admetus one jot more than was nominated in the bond. Thus he refused the offer, from Chicago University, of the full salary of a professor for lectures during one quarter each year: a single quarter was too much. Of course the price of such devotion was poverty. His method was to labor at teaching or hack-writing until he had accumulated a little money, and then to live on it as simply as possible as long as it lasted, too happy in composition to mind small discomforts. That it lasted longer in Europe than at home was one reason of his frequent voyages. Fortunately he did not need a large income. Aside from a barbaric fondness for jewelry and fancy waistcoats his personal tastes were inexpensive; though fond of the society of cultivated people, he had not the least trace of snobbery; almost his only financial luxury was the help he often extended to relatives and friends less prosperous than himself. Even with these advantages, however, he showed, it seems to me, a clear-headedness in the discrimination between immediate and ultimate values, and a stanch courage in the refusal to let the nearer interfere with the greater, as difficult to attain, and as rare, as they are admirable and worthy of emulation.

INTRODUCTION

The entire freedom of his work from the influences of commercialism, even in its most insidious and seductive forms, is due, I am sure, to this faculty he had of keeping money-earning and art as completely separated in his mind as they are in reality. It was placed in such striking relief by the circumstances, unprecedented in his hitherto obscure life, surrounding the production of "The Great Divide" in the autumn of 1906 (the single decisive worldly success of his short career) that I remember vividly what he told me of his affairs during a brief visit in the country soon after the opening night. He was then earning about five hundred dollars a week from the play, and was besieged by reporters, publishers, managers, and general social invitations. He was also quite unspoiled by it all, as simple in manner and cordial in talk as ever, and more enthusiastic over the beauties of the country than over the glories of Broadway. In the course of a long morning walk he told me that he hoped sometime to be able to buy a farm, where he could write undisturbed, and that now for the first time, among those New England hills, he realized how he had been tempted by large offers, received from four different publishers, for "The Great Divide" in novel form. Such sums had been mentioned as twenty-five, and even fifty, thousand dollars. But it had always seemed to him, he said, that the turning of a play into a novel, or *vice versa*, was a confounding of two essentially diverse types of art, and therefore a violation of a basic artistic principle; and he had refused all the offers.

INTRODUCTION

Not that there was anything of the prig in him — his sympathies were far too broad for that. The notes in which he discusses with Mr. Gilder the suppression of his initials on the poem written in his honor reveal a characteristic mingling of modesty as to his own attainments with delight in the appreciation of others and tender concern for their feelings. He had, too, that rarest form of humor which enables a man to laugh at himself, and an artist to relish parodies of his own style. We see it in the letter of January 24, 1901, to Mr. Edwin Arlington Robinson, in which he plays with the notion of how his "florid vocabulary" may affect a brother poet of the opposed method, a devotee of under-statement. Even in college days, when some solemnity of egotism is almost the accepted attitude, he had already this self-immolating humor. A college mate, I remember, used to make fun of the "foolish little cricket thing" in the song, "My love is gone into the East,"[1] and to turn the third stanza into baldest prose by the simple device of changing "or late or soon" into "sooner or later." That Moody may have been a little nettled as well as amused is suggested by his request, when he sent me "Dawn Parley" a year or two later, that before reading it I abstract myself for twelve hours from the society of the jester; but all the same he thoroughly enjoyed the joke, and recurs to it with unction in his letter of December 1, 1895. When he was writing "Gloucester Moors," at East Gloucester, in the spring of 1900, he asked a lady at the hotel,

[1] "Poems and Plays," vol. I, p. 151.

learned in wild-flowers, to tell him the names of all she
knew, and used some of them in the second stanza —

> "Jill o'er the ground is purple blue,
> Blue is the quaker-maid."

One item in the catalogue, baby blue-eye, brought
from him a shout of laughter, and the suggestion that
it ought to be incorporated in the line

> "Baby blue is the baby blue-eye."

In the long run, and after all analysis, it is Moody's
broad humanity that stands out as the most lovable
trait of the man and the imperishable quality in the
poet. He accepted human nature, and glorified it. He
pitied its fallibility and admired its aspiration; and he
identified himself with it, frankly recognizing in his
own character the two conflicting elements. From one
of his most serious letters, to a friend who does not
wish it to be published entire, the following passage
may be taken as a touching illustration: —

"Thanks for your word of cheer. It found me in a
state of dejection compounded of grippe and unfaith-
fulness, and lifted me to the heights again — the only
climate that suits my lungs these days, though the
valleys with their lights and business are tempting
when night sets in, and too often betray me downward.
. . . I needed the good word you sent me more than a
little, and am in your debt a trifle deeper than before —
if a matter of a few thousands is worth counting in
my hopeless insolvency. If my work, stumbling and

delayed as it usually seems to me, gives you any help in the contemplation, consider what the candour and spiritual grace of your character have been and are to me, looking with eyes no less wistful after righteousness for being somewhat bleared and dazzled by sensuous strayings. These things are perhaps best left unsaid, but now and then one forgets that he is an Anglo-Saxon and remembers only that he is a man, with a man's eternal aims, and a man's chances of help and hindrance on the tragic road; for which former it is not unbecoming from time to time to give thanks somewhat soberly."

Such a passage as this evokes for us afresh, and with an even more intimate sense of personal presence, the generous nature that has expressed this religion of humanity with incomparable power in Raphael's hymn to man in Act III of the "Masque of Judgment." Deeply spiritual, and as far as possible removed from the sensualism the thoughtless have found in it, is his paganism, as there set forth, his belief in the feelings, the passions, and the senses. He conceives them all as ministers of spirituality, and sees them transfigured in that ministration. He believes that through them alone is spirituality realized, or realizable.

"Not in vain, not in vain,"

sings Raphael, —

> "The spirit hath its sanguine stain,
>   And from its senses five doth peer
>   As a fawn from the green windows of a wood."

INTRODUCTION

To his mind the only possible attitude was a hearty acceptance of life as a whole. He was an enemy of nothing that is positive, but only of the negative things: doubt, cowardice, indifference, all ascetic denials of life. The reader of the letters that follow will, it is hoped, come ever more clearly to recognize the warm-hearted, welcoming personality that speaks in them. He was one of the few who can use, in their fullest sense, the words he has put into the mouth of Raphael: —

> "O struggler in the mesh
>   Of spirit and of flesh
> Some subtle hand hath tied to make thee Man,
>
> . . . .
>
> My bosom yearns above thee at the end,
> Thinking of all thy gladness, all thy woe;
>   Whoever is thy foe,
>   I am thy friend, thy friend."

D. G. M.

New York, April, 1913.

SOME LETTERS OF
William Vaughn Moody

SOME LETTERS OF
𝔚illiam 𝔙aughn 𝔐oody

IN spite of his habitual extreme reticence about personal and family affairs, Moody once confided to me that when, in the fall of 1889, he entered Harvard College, his entire capital consisted of twenty-five dollars.[1] He was also partly responsible for the support of one of his sisters, I believe; though his statements were always so vague on these points that even after knowing him years one was never surprised at the sudden cropping up in his conversation of a hitherto uncatalogued relative. Certain it is that he worked hard at typewriting, tutoring, proctoring, — anything he could find to do, meanwhile studying to such good purpose that at the end of the third year he had enough points for graduation. He accordingly spent his senior year abroad, tutoring a boy in order to earn his way. It was at this time that he made the first of his many visits to Greece. The winter he spent chiefly in Florence.

During his undergraduate years at Cambridge he had contributed some verse to the *Harvard Monthly*, and

---

[1] William Vaughn Moody was born July 8, 1869, at Spencer, Indiana.

3

he continued these contributions during his travels and after his return to Cambridge as a graduate student and instructor. Other *Harvard Monthly* poets of his day were Philip Henry Savage, also of the class of 1893, Hugh McCulloch (1892), and, a little earlier, Dr. George Santayana (1886). In the later class of 1895 was graduated his friend Joseph Trumbull Stickney, of whose posthumous book of poems he was one of the editors.

To Robert Morss Lovett

[Sept. 5, 1892.]

WARWICK. [ENGLAND.]

DEAR ROBERT:

We arrived here yesterday (Sept. 4) after a charming two weeks in the Scotch and English lakes, and expect to remain for ten days or so. I hope that you and Dow can get in your English trip before we leave Warwickshire, so that I can give you the benefit of my accumulated experience in dealing with the Insolent Briton and in viewing the historic monuments of his insolence. These midland counties are excellently beautiful, to use Mr. Howells's solemn phrase, and beautiful in a fresh wide-awake way which will appeal to you doubly after the sultry splendor of Italy. . . .

WILL M——.

WILLIAM VAUGHN MOODY

To Robert Morss Lovett
[Paris, October, 1892.]

DEAR ROBERT:

Will you add another star to the crown the Lord keeps for those who waver not in friendship, by receiving the package of books which I send by this mail, paying the custom-house charges (if there are any) and forwarding the package to the address below? . . .

I hope to receive the Monthly regularly. Am sorry not to send anything for the October number. I have turned Pegasus out to pasture and he eateth much green grass, but inclineth not to soar. . . .

To Robert Morss Lovett
[Paris, Nov. 22, 1892.]

DEAR ROBERT:

Please receive my heartfelt thanks for the telegram, the book-forwarding, the rank list and the assessment notice. . . . After all sorts of persuasion, physical and moral, the rank list refuses to disgorge more than five A's for me, which leaves me with only thirteen and a half toward a *summa*. I fear even your professional aplomb will be staggered by the hopelessness of the situation.

5

So far I have had little time and no inclination for study, but under the sedative influence of German beer and German beauties I hope to get my pulses down to a pace where grinding will be a delirious adventure. We have been in Paris now seven weeks and I have learned this dainty Sodom tolerably well, I flatter myself. I dare say your fingers are reaching instinctively after your blue pencil, to put the mark of eternal damnation on my adjective. But I insist on dainty. After three or four nights spent with "les gens qui s'amusent" in some of the places where a fortunate acquaintance with a French officer gave me entrance, I am sure that never in the history of man was the scarlet robe so delicately woven or of so gossamer a texture. I send a piece of verse — for which, I fear, your blue pencil will have the same horrible affinity. Read it yourself first and let not mercy season justice. If it is printed I should like to have a proof if possible. . . .

WILL.

To Robert Morss Lovett

[DRESDEN: April 11, 1893.]

DEAR ROBERT:

I was overjoyed to find a letter from you waiting for me in Dresden, doubly so as I had had no mail since leaving Italy, six weeks before. We were unfortunately prevented from accepting the Grand Llama's invitation, but made up for it in part by hobnobbing with the Sultan in Constantinople, the quality of whose wine and rose-leaf jelly is absolutely beyond criticism. We had the good luck to strike some of the Lord's people on leaving Italy, Mr. Edward Lowell and family, and spent three weeks with them in Greece — three weeks of flawless enjoyment for me, in spite of the resin in the wine and the ubiquitous prowling of the Philistine. After doing what could be easily done from Athens, — Eleusis, Phylae, Aegina, and Marathon, — we went down to Nauplia in the Peloponnesus, and made flying trips to Epidaurus, Argos and Mycenae. Instead of coming into Germany by way of Triest we chose the Aegean route, and spent a week in Constantinople, studying the mind and manners of ye sad-eyed Mussulman. So that my time has been pretty well taken up for a long time, and your rebuke on the subject of letterwriting is only half merited, or at least so I try to believe for ease of conscience sake. Two belated and badly-battered Monthlies have reached me — the October and January numbers, I think, but aside from this and a newspaper clipping now and then, Harvard and her doings have been pure conjecture for me. I am sorry not to have been able to send anything for padding, but I have had neither time nor inclination to write. The outline of Italian II came to hand all right and I am infinitely obliged. I have put all my spare time on Dante so far, and probably shall not try now to work up Sheldon's course — I have not the nerve to throw such sand in the maw of the faculty Cerberus, lest he should turn and rend me. These days I suck much milk from the paps of the Wagnerian muse, so far without any symptoms of spiritual colic — Walküre and Tannhäuser last week, with a prospect of the whole Rheingold cycle next. Your flashlight description of the meeting of the church in Laodicea was most picturesque and made me horribly homesick for such communion — whether God is blackballed or not I am a candidate for the first vacant position as usher or organ-boy. Also the Italian restaurant à la Luino wrung my bowels with envious longings of a curious gastro-psychic complexity. We sail from Genoa May 24, and shall be in Boston by the 5th or 6th of June, so that I can attend to everything but the gown, which I

8

would be glad if you would order for me according to the enclosed measurements. I have applied for a fellowship for next year, and if I get it shall come back for an indefinite period. I hope you will be a doorkeeper still, even if Providence has n't the good taste to make you a burner of myrrh before the inmost altars. . . . I have about decided not to spread on Class-day, as it is a huge bother and being away all year has kept me clear of social debts. Do you think it advisable to spread under the circumstances? . . . As ever,

WILL.

Of Moody's undergraduate verse there is little if any that he, as an artist, would care to have preserved. His Class Day Poem, however, called "The Song of the Elder Brothers," has an autobiographical interest that justifies the quotation of a few stanzas here. All through his life the contrast between the fresh vitality of the west and the mellower civilization of the east exercised his imagination; as a man he felt it strongly in coming from his Indiana village to Harvard, and later to Florence and Greece; as an artist he tried at various times to picture it, notably in "The Great Divide." The class day poem shows that in his undergraduate years he was already keenly aware of the quality of Harvard, and what is more, conscious of his personal debt to its traditions.

The nucleus of the poem is the song in praise and thanksgiving to Alma Mater which the poet attributes to his spiritual "elder brothers," to all those who before him

> "Saw the looming of the gates
> That open unto larger seas,
> Who heard the singing of the breeze
> That calls to sweeter, lonelier fates.
>
> . . . .
>
> Longfellow, with the blossomed hair
> And low-tuned lyre, who sings alway:
> 'Behind the cloud is golden day,
> So let us fare as children fare.'
>
> And Emerson, who stops and hears
> The pine trees' ancient overtones,
> Who listens at the hearts of stones,
> And weighs the star-dust and the years.
>
> . . . .
>
> And all the other men who brought
> Some message from beyond the bar
> Of sense, where ever chime and jar
> The opalescent seas of thought."

After describing the song of these elder brothers, and asking what answer we who "kneel now before the mother's face" shall send, he continues: —

> "Shall we not say: 'While sunset flings
> Through our great hall its jewelled rain,

10

WILLIAM VAUGHN MOODY

From windows blazoned with their train
Of poets, saints, and soldier kings,

So long shall this our college throw
Across the loud noon, bare and bright,
A jewelled and a sunset light,
A many-ribboned golden glow.

While Charles's chivalry doth shine
Upon the pane, her halls shall hold
Such hearts as gave up land and gold
And went to die in Palestine.

.   .   .   .

So long as Homer clasps his lyre
Among us some shall still be found,
About whose brows the gods have wound
Song's amaranthine buds of fire.

While Shakespeare waits and seems to scan
Each form that passes in the dusk,
One here shall break away the husk
Which hides the fruit-sweet heart of man.'

So shall we answer, kneeling low,
Feeling the time draw very near
To part, and common things grow dear,
And things forgotten clearer grow.

Long, mellow twilights in the Yard,
The peace that settles from the trees,
The tinkle of guitars, the leas
Of laughter dripping sweet as nard;

The lazy Charles at noon; the long
Salt meadows; the slow beat of oars;
Faint cheery calls; across the moors
The great tower rising like a song:

Till we can only bow the head,
Waiting the Mother's gracious ken,
And reach across the years to when
We, too, may say as those have said:

'Fair Harvard! Mother fair and grand!
Behold, we are thy children too;
Great mother from whose breast we drew
The larger strength of brain and hand!

Lo, have we borne a knightly sword?
Thy kiss was misty on the blade!
Lo, men's hearts have we stirred and swayed?
Thou puttest in our mouth the word!'"

The year after his graduation Moody spent in study at Cambridge, eking out a slender income by the editorial labors on Bulfinch's Mythology with Mr. Lovett to which the letters refer, and in other ways. Then came a year as instructor in English composition under his friend Professor Lewis E. Gates, and in the spring of 1895 the summons to Chicago University which took him thither in the following fall.

During his two graduate years at Harvard he wrote a good many poems, but they were for the most part immature and more or less imitative of Keats, Rossetti, Walt Whitman, and especially Browning. Although he profited much from the writing of them, especially in his rhythms, eventually so marvellous in their subtlety and variety, he considered most of them only studies, as is shown by his omitting them from the " Poems " of 1901.

To Robert Morss Lovett

DEAR ROBERT:

As you purpose returning so soon, I think I will not come to Waterville, as the present stringency in the money market has at last crippled even my immense resources. Do not hurry back on Bulfinch's account, however; I will have a general supervision over Zeus's amours, and will keep Heré out of his hair until such time as the color fadeth out of the Waterville sky and the dregs in the wine cup grow bitter. Till then, farewell.

WILL M——.

CAMBRIDGE,
Aug. 10, 1893.

To Robert Morss Lovett

DEAR ROB:

. . . .

What became of the Seal Harbor Coeducational Trust? I have heard nothing of it and am consumed with curiosity. My two weeks' taste of the

13

World's Fake has left upon my lips the salt of vanities. I long even for a swallow of Laodicean shaving water to cool my tongue. Hoping to indulge with you in that mild beverage before long,

As ever,　　　WILL.

CAMBRIDGE,
　September 17, 1893.

To Robert Morss Lovett

23 HILTON.
[CAMBRIDGE, Feb. 5, 1894.]

DEAR ROB:

The midyears [examinations] have left me limp as a rag, and have convinced me that, instead of an amiable divorce such as you suggest, Philology and Minerva are destined to part with mutual scorn and vituperation, if indeed their feud does not result in pistols and pillow-chokings. If you want to rescue either of them you must come on in March as you promise, for I will not answer for their lives a day later than the twentieth. Joking aside, though, we all expect you then, and are already beginning to plan revels, masques, and pageants of royal magnificence to fleet the time withal.

· · · · · · · · ·

14

WILLIAM VAUGHN MOODY

Stone and Kimball . . . are getting out volumes of verse for Mac and Santy [Hugh McCulloch and George Santayana] and have even approached *me* with harp and psaltery, though so far I have had grace from God to resist their blandishments. Cambridge is rather good fun this winter. The Browning Club, I hear, still leads a subterranean existence somewhere, but its place in the upper world has been taken by the "Folk-lore Society," an organization much affected by voluptuous young ladies yearning to walk in the cold clear light of science. They are all saturated with sun-myths, and ghosts, trolls, and witches are their daily walk and conversation. My frightened attempts to be statistical have been frowned upon, and I fear I shall not be a success. Mrs. Toy still takes pity on my orphan state, and asks me to see interesting people at her house. Last Friday I bearded a whole den of lions at Mrs. Moulton's — from old Dr. Holmes to Robert Grant and old Trowbridge — to say nothing of an Oxford prof who has dined with Dodo at the Master of Balliol's. Do you have any time for writing? Do not bury your talent in a napkin — even if the napkin stands for domestic bliss and the ground for the goodliness of this

15

world. Do make your plans to come on during the spring vacation: we refuse to be refused. . . .

WILL.

Feb. 5, 1894.

To Robert Morss Lovett

23 HILTON'S BLOCK.
CAMBRIDGE.

. . . .

I don't know whether you know that I have decided to shuffle about next year in your old shoes — with Gates in English 22. I should hesitate to accept it did I not have such splendid examples before my eyes of gorgeous scholastic butterflies hatched from this dull cocoon.

. . . .

June 21, 1894.

To Daniel Gregory Mason

ENDION COTTAGE,
LONG LAKE, N. Y.
[Postmarked: July 21, 1894.]

DEAR DAN:

Your somewhat hysterical note reached me just as I was leaving Cambridge, and since I reached this loafer's paradise I have melted into a spiritual

16

jelly fish, with a corresponding amount of energy for letter writing or any other occupation of civilized man. I sleep by the week, eat by the tub-full, and never have an idea from one day's end to another. The hotel, which is a mile up the lake, is full of a dull spawn, only human by virtue of being made in the likeness of an outraged God. My single encounter with the sex has not bristled with poetry, for though I sat with her an hour every attempt at self-revelation on her part was met by my exclamation, unuttered but passionate, "O brisky juvenal, and eke most lovely Jew!" Finding no earthly lips to breathe fire into the clay of my longing, I lie doggedly on my back under the pines and wait the descent of the goddess. Heaven send her soon, or I shall be past kissing! To do the place justice though, it is very beautiful, and only needs a remotely adequate Comer to pant through the blueness[1] in order to put me in direct communication with Helicon and Castaly.

I suppose you are swimming through rose-colored seas of song, with wan breasts glimmering

[1] "Come then, complete incompletion, O comer,
Pant through the blueness, perfect the summer!"
BROWNING: "Wanting is — what?"

up toward your amorous lips — in other words that you have no end of a cinch on Apollo and are as much one of Venus's cosseted darlings as you bade fair to be when I left you. Please keep me informed concerning the various stages of your nearness to ——'s soul. I presume you realize what sort of a risk you run, and in view of our talk about direct and indirect passion it would be supererogatory for me to hint at my firm conviction that the young lady in question is deeply conversant with the fact that a straight line is the shortest distance between two points, and that if you propose to work out any little problems in spiritual geometry with her, you will have to accept the theorem.

All my plans of work have crumbled away; I simply lie and cumber the earth, outrageously contented. I feel myself drifting toward the damnable heresy that the unlit lamp and the ungirt loin[1] have their advantages. Can't you throw me a rope in the shape of a lyric idea? I should not know what to do with it, but it would comfort me.

Beseechingly,

W. V. M.

[1] "And the sin I impute to each frustrate ghost
Is — the unlit lamp and the ungirt loin."
    BROWNING: "The Statue and the Bust."

WILLIAM VAUGHN MOODY
(1894)

WILLIAM VAUGHN MOODY

To Robert Morss Lovett

ENDION COTTAGE,
LONG LAKE, N. Y.
[July, 1894.]

DEAR ROB:

Your letter reached me just as I was leaving Cambridge for this hole in the Adirondacks, where myself and my sister propose to sleep the summer away. It is a stunning place as far as natural beauty is concerned, but as yet not even a remotely adequate Comer has consented to pant through the blueness. Besides the deer and the bears there is nothing to commune with, and the single social resource is a hotel a mile up the lake, where polypous New Yorkers vaguely swarm. Accordingly there is no excuse for me if I do not do some good work in one line or another, but I greet my opportunity listlessly, with an unlit lamp and an ungirt loin, and simply lie under the pine trees and cumber the earth in a state of outrageous content. I deeply commiserate you, if you propose to stay in that hell's kitchen all summer "dribbling biographical details and cheap criticism." Your outlook on the teacher's mission does not seem pregnantly optimistic. I was glad to hear that Bulfinch is so near completion — the thing must have been a vile bother. . . .

I hope you will cleave to the plan of coming east in September. We will have that dinner at Marliave's which missed fire last spring and drink a bottle of Chianti to the forgetting of sorrows.

W. V. M.

To Mrs. C. H. Toy

CAMP ENDION.
LONG LAKE, N. Y.
[August, 1894.]

DEAR MRS. TOY:

. . . Three bears have been shot on the borders of the lake since we came, one of them on the spot where we had picnicked the day previous. For a decadent spirit, a bewildered moth about the candle of latter-day Illumination, I maintain this is getting pretty near to Nature's naked bosom.

Indeed, the forest is no toy forest, but rustles and billows away on every hand in miles on miles of reverberant color. I can do nothing with it. Its brutal mindlessness, its huge *insouciance*, awes and humiliates me. It has a way of looking over your head with a gay and ferocious oblivion of your interesting personality that puts you out

20

of countenance. As you lie on your back under these gigantic pines and listen to the inarticulate multitudinous life of the thing, you find yourself reversing the Fichtean telescope, and coming reluctantly to believe that perhaps God could manage to think his thoughts without pouring himself through just your highly ingenious brain. I did not know to be sure that the contrary conviction was at the base of all my thinking, until the negation of it was thus thrust into my face — but so it is, and the experience is desperately debilitating. I have developed a crooning fondness for the Zeitgeist, now that it looks like a fever-clot in the eternal brain, and as I begin to suspect that the voice of many prophets prophesying is as the noon-fly and the strident midge to vex the ears and eyes of God.

. . . .

To Robert Morss Lovett

43 GRAY'S,
CAMBRIDGE.

DEAR ROB:

I am in a tight place and need a little money to tide me over till the Harvard goose begins to lay her meagre eggs. Can you lend me fifty on our

Bulfinch expectations? I feel very mean to ask for it, but being in a hole is being in a hole, and the situation transcends philosophy. I shall want it for a couple of months at the longest.

In haste,

W. V. M.

Sept. 27, 1894.

If you are short yourself, you wont hesitate to confess, of course.

To Robert Morss Lovett

43 GRAY'S,
CAMBRIDGE.
[October, '94.]

DEAR ROB:

Your note, with enclosed check, reached me yesterday. The aptness of old Bulfinch's remittance (was Bulfinch the Book or the Man? My concepts concerning him have acquired a mythic vagueness) — the aptness of the remittance, I say, is such as to give a factitious and theatrical tinge to the transaction. I hope you have not tampered with the Facts of History, for it is comforting to think that the ravens still come so opportunely to feed the hungering prophet. I had quite made up my mind not to take any of the proceeds, as your work on the book after I left it must have far exceeded my own little scissorings and pastings, but necessity is the mother of lies, and I accept as brazenly as if it was my due, not however, without a surreptitious pang of gratitude. . . .

As always,

W. V. M.

To Robert Morss Lovett

43 GRAY'S HALL.
CAMBRIDGE.

DEAR ROB:

You will forgive me for not sooner answering your kind letter, when you call to mind your early morning and midnight coping with the English 22 fortnightly. After a long season of prayer and watching, I feel that I must turn a deaf ear to your alluring invitation, and have written Herrick definitely declining the position. I do this with a full realization of how much I am giving up, both materially and spiritually. I am sure that an experience of Chicago life would have been a good thing for me, and it goes without saying that the renewed companionship would have been no end jolly. At the same time, there are other considerations, which I have set forth at length in my letter to Herrick and will not bore you by repeating here, which make it clear to me that I should remain here next year, and accept the instructorship which Hill offers me, with a prospect, dim perhaps but cherishable, of pinching a fellowship at the end of it. The message which Miss Mott-Smith was gracious enough to couple with yours lends an added pang to the renunciation, but I must be strong to heed not. With sincerest gratitude for your kindness in the matter and as sincere regret that I cannot now see my way clear to joining you in spreading the gospel of sweetness and light, I remain

Faithfully yours,
W. V. M.

April 25, 1895.

To Robert Morss Lovett

43 GRAY'S HALL,
CAMBRIDGE.

DEAR ROB:

. . . .

I have called several times on Damon without finding him at home. Hill, I believe, has spoken

to him about the Chicago position, and I believe
he is very likely to accept it if it is offered him.
He is, in my opinion, the best man for your purposes now at Harvard, with the possible exception of Young, to whom the Rajah has also tentatively broached the subject. I know less about
Young myself, but he is in high favor here among
the undergraduates, and enjoys, I understand,
the light of the Rajah's countenance. I have
compunctious visitings every now and then, as
I think of the friendly time we might have had
together next year. You will, however, dwell only
sporadically upon this earth, and I could not follow you, except by way of imaginative sympathy,
into the interstellar spaces which will be your
real abiding-place — whence comes abatement of
the pang of renunciation. I hope you will make
your visit east as early as possible that we may
have a few days' usufruct of you before your
wings sprout.

. . . .

Hastily,

WILL.

May 9, 1895.

To Robert Morss Lovett

43 GRAY'S HALL,
CAMBRIDGE.

DEAR ROB:

You are immensely kind to bestow upon me the honors of groomsmanship. I accept with delight, duly tempered with a sense of my unworthiness. I have today received a letter from my people which changes the outlook for me somewhat, as it makes it necessary for me to reap a larger harvest of shekels than I have any immediate prospect of doing here. If you have not as yet made an offer of the Chicago position to any one else could you possibly hold it open until you come East? Do not think of doing so if it involves any risk or inconvenience on either your part or Herrick's, but if you are both willing, I should be glad. I hope you will not think I take an altogether mercenary view of the situation: you must take the spiritual sub-intention for granted. I shall write Herrick to-day, if I can bring myself to brave the scorn which my tergiversation will merit at his hands.

Faithfully,

May 18, 1895. W. V. M.

WILLIAM VAUGHN MOODY

On July 3, 1895, Moody and I sailed for Europe, landing on the 15th at Antwerp, where we were joined for a short trip through Brussels, Ghent, Bruges, Lille, Amiens, and Beauvais by Professor Gates. Moody's delight in the beauty of the cathedrals, the picturesqueness of the landscapes, and the bits of talk with peasants, servants, and railway acquaintances which he never failed to snatch, was a constant pleasure. The easy transitions his mind made from poetic feeling and imagery to the broadest colloquial humor made him an incomparable companion. At Amiens, for example, he calls the delicate rose-window of the cathedral "God's spiderweb"; at Comines, on the border of France, charmed with the pure French of the waitress, he asks the names of all the viands, and in return communicates that the English name of raspberry jam is "Red-goo," and with a solemnity that convulses us watches her efforts to reproduce it, with much rolling of the R.

On the 26th, Mr. Gates having left for Paris, we started on a short walking tour through Brionne, l'Hotellerie, Lisieux, Caen, Saint-Lo, Tessy, and Vire. At Caen, on a rainy afternoon, Moody made the first sketch of the poem which eventually, after much revision, became "Jetsam." At Tessy-sur-Vire we were awakened before dawn one morning by the bugles of a regiment passing up one of the narrow streets — a valorous music strangely impressive in that darkness and silence. Moody has commemorated it in the speech of the Third Youth in Act IV of the "Masque of Judgment":

"But always ere the dayspring took the sky,
Somewhere the silver trumpets were acry, —
Sweet, high, oh, high and sweet!
What voice could summon so but the Soul's Paraclete?
Whom should such voices call but me, to dare and die?
O ye asleep here in the eyrie town,
Ye mothers, babes, and maids, and aged men,
The plain is full of foe-men! Turn again —
Sleep sound, or waken half
Only to hear our happy bugles laugh
Lovely defiance down,
As through the steep
Grey streets we sweep,
Each horse and man a ribbéd fan to scatter all that chaff!"

Under date August 26th I find in my journal the following entry:

"Boat [Rouen] to Caudebec; thence to Yvetot on foot; thence to Havre. Met on the open road an old man dressed very meagrely, with slippers open at the toes, ragged shirt, and bare head, who lifted his hands eloquently, and chanted to the empty landscape:

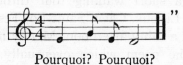

Pourquoi? Pourquoi?

This experience was the germ of the poem, "Old Pourquoi," written many years later.

We returned to America in September, and he immediately went to Chicago and began work as an instructor in the English Department of Chicago University.

WILLIAM VAUGHN MOODY

To Robert Morss Lovett

BOSTON,
Sept. 17, 1895.

DEAR ROB:

I reached home yesterday and am stopping
here a few days to get my books packed, after
which I shall make my descent on Chicago. I
should reach the University Friday afternoon or
Saturday morning next. Can you secure me or
suggest to me a temporary abiding-place, from
the vantage shelter of which I may survey the
field of battle, learn the rudiments of tactic and
become conversant with the bristling vocabulary
of arms?

. . . .

Will telegraph or write when I decide upon a
train, but do not take the trouble to be at home
on my advent. You could leave the suggestion as
to boarding house prominently posted to catch
my hungering eye.

In haste,

W. V. M.

39 Commonwealth Ave.

SOME LETTERS OF

To Josephine Preston Peabody

MY DEAR MISS PEABODY:

I have put off sending you the verses with the naïve thought of using them for a link between the old Cambridge life and this new one. Scoff at my superstition, but do not too scornfully entreat the pathetic little versicle of a bond-bearer, shivering with the double knowledge of the portentous mission and his own objective comicality. Cambridge — mellow and autumnal — begins already to take on really mythic colors — to loom symbolic, under the stress of this relentless prairie light and vast featureless horizon. I begin to believe that your charge against me of theatricality was just — that all my life there in the east was a sort of tragi-farce, more or less consciously composed, so rudely awake and in earnest is everything here. . . .

I do not know what this place is going to do for me, but am sure of its potency — its alchemical power to change and transmute. It is appallingly ugly for one thing — so ugly that the double curtain of night and sleep does not screen the aching sense. For another thing it is absorbing — crude juice of life — intellectual and social protoplasm.

WILLIAM VAUGHN MOODY

Far aloft hovers phantom Poetry, no longer my delicate familiar. But I dream of another coming of hers, a new companionship more valorous and simple-hearted.

. . . .

CHICAGO UNIVERSITY
Sept. 22, 1895.

To Daniel Gregory Mason

[CHICAGO,
October 2, 1895.]

Your letter came yesterday, with cheek on the smooth cheek of another — a friendlier pair nor a tunefuller ever stretched wing together. Riding to town on some sort of transfigured chariot that whilom was a railway car, I perused them. Rest of morning spent shopping in the New Jerusalem, walking on golden pavements, and interwarbling on the theme of shirts and socks with whatever seraphic creatures had found it good that day to put on the habit and estate of shop-girls for the glory of God and the furtherance of his kingdom. Returning, the lake allured me — one topaz. Re-reading of letters. Throbbing of the topaz heart: opening and shutting of the sunlight: bursting to bloom of some sudden impalpable enveloping flower of the air, with the scent thereof. The twentieth century dates from yesterday, and we are its chosen; if not as signs set in the heavens of its glory, at least as morning birds that carolled to it, mindless of the seductive and quite palpable worm.

More later — brutally busy.

W——

To Daniel Gregory Mason

[CHICAGO,
October 23, 1895.]

DEAR DAN:

I have so far made but miserly return for that bully long letter you wrote in the purpureal flush of reconciliation and renascent duality — or let me say, and try to think, trinity — with the Bard. If you knew the beast Chicago, the pawing and glaring of it, you would not find me hard to forgive. I have been in the condition of the *Kluger Schneiderlein* in the bear-pit: it has taken all my frightened dexterity to keep out of the jaws of the creature. Now that I have learned its ways a trifle, and can make it crack my nuts and dance to my fiddling, the first use I make of my loosened faculties is to beg forgiveness for past

shortcoming, and plead for more letters. I am
eager to know how you find Dvořák, whether
New York keys you up or spiritually ham-strings
you, whether the fair, the chaste, the inexpressive
She has throbbed out of the circumambient
nebula; what you and the Muse find to talk about
under the sheets, now you are decently married
— of all of which and much more I demand an
immediate and circumstantial report.

For my own part I have been having a highly
exciting time. I have two classes — one of forty,
the other of twenty — nearly two-thirds of whom
are girls. Picture my felicity when I inform you
that far from the frowsy, bedraggled, anemic,
simpering creatures I anticipated, half of them at
least are stars. I regret that popular usage should
have dechromatized the term, for I mean stars
of the most authentic stellarity and the most
convincing twinkle. Lecturing before them is like
a singing progress from Boötes to the Lyre, with
wayfaring worlds to lift the chorus. At the beginning I made an honest man's effort to talk about
the qualities of style and the methods of description, but I am a weak vessel. Now I drool bliss-
fully about God in his world, with occasional
wadings into spumy Styx and excursions into the

empyrean. My work has been heavier so far than
I fondly hoped it would be, and I can see little
chance ahead for sleeping on Latmos. I experience
aching diastoles,[1] however, and that is the great
thing to my thinking. To be a poet is a much
better thing than to write poetry — out here at
least, watched by these wide horizons, beckoned
to by these swift streamers of victorious sunset.
After the fall term my work will be lighter, then
I shall try a night out, on a bed of lunary.

I have just had a letter from ——, air rarified,
sky greyish, with half-hints of opal and dove's
breast, a confused twittering from the hedges, not
unpleasing. Tenuous, but tense, like a harp string
in the treble.

W. V. M.

To Josephine Preston Peabody

[Autumn, 1895.]

Tell you about it? Doth the wind know its
wound, wherefore it groaneth? It is only an
affliction of the stars, at least this recent bundle
of pangs; they are of those that eat the hearts

---

[1] A word we had borrowed from physiology — the dilatation
of the heart in beating — and used as a name for moods of spiritual
elation. See the Introduction.

of crazy-headed comets zigzaging across the
Zodiac. Doubtless the incontinent closing of the
moon-flower dailies left me more defenseless
against these malign astral inroads, but the root of
the matter is some sort of cosmic apoplexy or
ear-ache of which I happen to be the centre.
Τὸ Πᾶν has the falling-sickness or the everlasting
doldrums, and selects me to ache through — that
is all. If I were not precociously aware of the
devices of his Celestial Completeness I should
suppose quite simply that Chicago was boring
me to death, that my work was meaningless
drudgery, that the crowd of spiteful assiduous
nothings that keep me from It (Ah, the vague
sweet-shrouding mute arch vocable!) were tantalizing me into stupid rage, and stinging my eye-
balls into blindness of the light. When in moments
of weakness I transfer the blame for my inward
dissatisfaction and disarray to outward things, I
am on the point of trundling my little instructorial
droning-gear into Lake Michigan, and stepping
out west or south on the Open Road, a free man
by the grace of God, and a tramp by Rachel's
intercession. But of course I know that I should
only be changing garments, and that I should
wake up some fine night and find my hay-stack

bristling with just such goblin dissension as now swarms over my counter-pane. However, it is easy to stand dissension. Anything is better than that awful hush settling down on everything, as if Tò Πᾶν had suddenly discovered himself to be stuffed with sawdust, and lost interest in his own ends and appetites. And that silence your brave words have scared back. I really begin to think you are Wise, and to stand in awe of you. That is a more convincing presentment of the "transscendent identity," that which shows it casting its own brain on one side as a worn out accessory, holding its own heart in its hands to burn, like the angel in Dante's dream. I pay you the compliment of believing that you would be capable of that, and I find it illustrious, and with your gracious permission propose to set it for a sign, right at a cross-roads where I sometimes skulk belated, peering fearful-eyed for Hecate.

The truth of the matter is, I suppose, that I am dissatisfied to the point of desperation with the kind of life that is possible out here. I used to have days in the east when a hedge of lilac over a Brattle Street fence or a strenuous young head caught against a windy sweep of sunset on Harvard Bridge, filled me with poignant perceptions

of a freer life of sense and spirit, — and I was frequently vaguely unhappy over it. But after all
one had n't far to go before finding some refinement of feeling, some delicate arabesque of convention, to help make up for the lack of liberty.
Out here there is even less liberty (because less
thought) and there is nothing — or next to
nothing — to compensate. If my lines were cast
in other places, — even other places in this gigantic ink-blot of a town — I could make shift to
enjoy my breath. I should make a very happy
and efficient peanut-vender on Clark or Randolph
Street, because the rush and noise of the blood in
the city's pulse would continually solicit and
engage me. The life of a motor-man is not without
exhilarating and even romantic features, and an
imaginative boot-black is lord of unskirted realms.
But out here, where there is no city life to gaze at,
nothing to relieve the gaseous tedium of a mush-
room intellectuality, no straining wickedness or
valiant wrestling with hunger to break the spectacle of Gospel-peddling comfort, — the imagination doth boggle at it!

· · · · · · · · · ·

SOME LETTERS OF

To Josephine Preston Peabody

[Probably Autumn, 1895.]

. . . .

Mr. Ruskin would not be happy in Chicago — God is a very considerable personage — So is Mr. Rockefeller — So am I, but for a different reason — Towers of Babel are out of fashion — Ride a Rambler — Four fifths of William Blake would not be accepted for publication by the Harvard Advocate — Life at a penny plain is d—d dear — Eat H. O. — The poet in a golden clime was born, but moved away early — A man may yearn over his little brothers and sisters and still be a good Laodicean — Art is not long, but it takes a good while to make it short — There will be no opera or steel engraving in the twentieth century — An angle-worm makes no better bait because it has fed on Cæsar — Wood fires are dangerous — So is life at a penny plain, but for a different reason — Towers of Babel, though out of fashion, are well received in Chicago — There were no birds in the Tower of Babel — God is a very considerable personage — So is Olga Nethersole — So are you, but for a different reason — I am owner of the spheres, and grow land-poor — Literature is a

38

fake and Nordau is its prophet — God bless McKinley — Love is not Time's fool: he was turned off for lack of wit — Eve was born before Ann Radcliffe, so the world goes darkling — Tom's a cold — I am old-rose, quoth 'a — God's pittykins 'ield ye, zany, for thy apple-greenness! 'T would gi' the Ding-an-Sich a colic to set eyes on 'e — Natheless Monet was a good painter, *and* color-blind —

W. V. M.

To Daniel Gregory Mason

DEC. 1, 1895.

MY DEAR DAN:

Day after crowded day I have looked at your delightful long letter, and said, in the sweet babble of the Little Cricket Thing,[1] that I would answer it sooner or later, when I was not as busy as hell. Then the speaking lines about your reclining on the Paderewskian bosom, arrived, with their tantalizing suggestion of dim-lighted rooms, transcendentalized rum toddy, and an auroral head uttering gold vaticination. I was jaundiced

---

[1] He refers to the parody by a Harvard friend, already mentioned, of some lines in his song "My love is gone into the East." See page xxv.

with jealousy for a week, thinking of the fulness
of your service before the great altars, and the
wretched scantlings of effort I was permitted
to give, standing afar off. To tell the truth, I
have n't the faintest splinter of sympathy for
the dolorousness of your condition, as set forth in
your letter. To be a runner of scales and to work
at canon and fugue by the job, strikes me as the
most enviable estate of man. Every scale you
run, every fugue you hammer out, is laying up
treasure in heaven — not by way of communal
walls and pavements only, but especially for the
house which your own winged self-ship shall
inhabit. I have as much respect for you as for
a disgruntled peach seed, which should cry out
against the lack of social opportunities in an
underground community. And besides the ultimate satisfaction, there is the daily delight of
pottering over your tools, trying their edge,
polishing their surfaces, feeling their delectable
ponderableness. No, you must go for comfort to
somebody who does n't have a sense of radiant
bien-être in fitting a new pen into a holder.

Which reminds me that, having a few hours
last week for ecstatic contemplation of my navel,
I emitted a more or less piercing yawp there-

concerning, in the form of a new treatment of the moon theme.[1] I have unfortunately bundled off the only copy to the Singer, so that I cannot send you the product, but if you are still interested you may ask her to pass it on to you. You will no doubt find much to dislike in it, but I hope that some of it may meet with your approval. You will recognize the elements drawn from that unforgettable night in the fields at Chartres. Having temporarily exorcised this particular demon, I am losing sleep over a project for a play, dealing with a character and a situation which seem to me intensely significant and eloquent, that of Slatter, the "New Mexico Messiah," who has been doing things in Denver of late. But I need not bother you with dough still in the kneading.[2]

. . . .

I am looking forward to some bully good talks at Christmas, and some good music at your expense, and a bottle of wine wherein we may drink to the meek brows of Her and It. Meanwhile, write.

WILL.

[1] The poem started in Caen the preceding summer. It eventually became "Jetsam."

[2] "The Faith Healer" did not, as a matter of fact, take on final shape until shortly before its author's death.

41

To Mary L. Mason

CHICAGO,
Dec. 12, 1895.

MY DEAR MRS. MASON,

You are wofully ignorant of the sweet uses of memory if you can picture me forgetting your delightful invitation to spend a fraction of my Christmas week at your home. . . .

Whisper it not in Gath, but I hunger and thirst after the East with a carnal longing. I thought I had relegated all you subtlety-spinning New Englanders to the limbo of the effete, where you were tolerantly allowed to exist and confuse economic relations only because you are, after all, rather nice. But of late, in the still watches, your niceness grows luminous and summoning. I still disapprove of you, but I want to see you very bad.

Expectantly,

WILLIAM VAUGHN MOODY.

To Josephine Preston Peabody

CHICAGO,
Dec. 15 [16?], 1895.

Just a word to tell you something of the immense good your letter did me. After I sent off the poem ["Jetsam"], the inevitable revulsion set in: I lost faith in it, and then, being in a state of nerves, took the easy step of losing faith in myself and the future. Still I kept hoping against hope that you would find a stray line to like and praise. When the days passed, and your silence pronounced gentle but final condemnation, I sat down and read the lines over. They had fallen dead ink. The paper dropped to the floor; I sat, elbows on desk and head in hands, and thought. I had felt the thing, I had put my best breath into the lines, and here they were, not only dead past hope, but graceless, repulsive, without the dignity or pathos of death. What then? For a long time I did not have heart squarely to face the issue — Life without that hope and solace, that pillar of smoke by day and of fire by night, — could I live it out so, in some sort of grey content? Outside my window the moon came out over the turbulent brute groping of the brown surge, walking in light as when she tormented the lowered eyes of Job, tempting him from Jehovah. She called me out with her, miles along the coast, and as I stumbled along in the vague light, gradually the mere effort I had made to say something of her wonder, began to seem its own justification.

When I came back the pages I gathered from the floor were farther than ever from adequacy, but somehow I cared for them, as one cares for a dead thing one picks up in the hedges, thinking of its brave fight for life. Then your letter came, and I read, stupidly at first, not understanding, your words of generous praise. I knew you were artist enough not to utter them merely for friendship's sake, and when I understood them, they filled me with joy which would have been out of all proportion to the matter at stake except that for me it was one of those mysterious pivotal small things on which the future turns silent and large. So you had actually liked it all, and were glad it had been done? Then it was not dead after all; my eyes had been seared? I read it through in the flush of pleasure and found it good, — absurdly, ravishingly good! So I took a deep breath, and sat down to write it over, with the sharp light of remembered disillusion on its weaknesses, and the memories of my night walk to beckon me on. I shall crave judgment on the result at Christmas, for I purpose to make a descent on Boston then, ravenous with a three-month's abstinence from subtlety-spinning. . . . I have . . . written to —— again. He has owed me a letter since September, but God knows who has the rights of this wretchedness, and of all our funny little Pantheon the absurd little god who gets the least of my service is the one labelled "Personal Dignity." I cannot think of any personal sacrifice I would not make to convince him of my friendship, or rather to establish once more the conditions which make friendship possible. I hope this does n't sound superior; it is not so meant.

W. V. M.

To Daniel Gregory Mason

Dec. 15, 1895.

1. Shall reach New York . . . Dec. 19.
2. Shall reach Boston . . . Dec. 26.
3. Must leave Boston . . . Dec. 31.
4. Shall leave Boston . . . God knows.

All except last date subject to change without notice.

W. V. M.

The hope of a vacation, expressed in the following letter in a characteristic metaphor, was illusory. Save for a ten-day bicycle trip with Mr. Schevill in the following June Moody seems to have stuck close to the "shop" for many months. In August he writes that he is to work all winter, in order to get a nine-months'

45

holiday beginning in the spring. In the letter of November 24 he speaks of having had "fourteen consecutive months of hack teaching," a statement which was not literally true, but which doubtless seemed true to his eager mind, always longing for fruitful leisure, fretful under drudgery. He eventually got away, as will be seen, in March, 1897.

To Mrs. C. H. Toy

CHICAGO,
Jan. 6, 1896.

MY DEAR MRS. TOY:

. . . It seemed very good to see a Cambridge face again, especially against this background of phantasmagoric ugliness. I long for something beautiful to look at with a really agonized and fleshly longing. My eye is horny with smoke and the outlines of grain elevators. But I must not enlarge upon my "state," since day is at hand. Looking up through the murk and the swaying shadow of seaweed I can just catch a hint of vanishing bubbles and green shattered needles of light. Two months more and I shall lift my encompassed head above the waters. Then off with the diving gear and ho for the groves of banyan and of cocoanut, and the little Injuns that grow between! . . .

46

WILLIAM VAUGHN MOODY

To Mary L. Mason

CHICAGO.
Jan. 11, 1896.

MY DEAR MRS. MASON,

I have postponed writing because I suspected you would rather have a letter written composedly out of a rising desire for talk or its substitute, than a hurried note setting forth with a prim gasp that I had got here with no broken bones. I have not quite got accustomed to the raw bite of things again, after humoring my skin with the delicate eastern impingements. Indeed I have been since getting back as helpless a victim to the blue devils as it is in my temperament ever to be. The gross result of the life one can lead in a place like this is satisfactory enough, but the net result, the fine slow-oozing crystal distillation, is tragically small — and I fancy that for such as I the unsublimated mass must always keep a disheartening suggestion. The enervating thing about the place is its shallow kindness. People are so eager to give you credit for virtues that you do not possess that you feel ashamed to put forth those that are yours. Then when you do take heart of grace, and do or say or think a really good thing, and win the facile applause, you have a bad taste in the mouth to think that any jigster's trick would have won you the same magnificent triumph. I sigh, like the ancient worthy, for a stern friend, one who will not be gulled by any thimble-rig sophistry, who will puncture with sweet skepticism my little soap-bubble eloquences, and by so doing give me heart to try and be wise. I recognize of course that the wish is a weak one, that I ought to be my own detective, gendarme, judge, and hangman; and I have made some flabby efforts to execute these functions upon myself, but so far with indifferent success. Do you think a wife would do any good? I have cast appalled glances at that ultimate rigor of self-discipline, but my eyes have been blest by no reassuring light. Something I must have to key life up, to give it musical pitch and the knit coherence of music. If I were free I could get all that out of my little gift and great passion for the poet's craft, but hampered as I am by intellectual drudgery that is only one burden more, and adds the last note of poignancy to the tedium of the days. I have lately thought with envy amounting to wickedness of D——'s complete service of the thing that seems to him real under the sun: if he were not so dear, I could find it in my heart to hate him cordially for it.

Another thing that afflicts my soul is the delicate strange winter light that lies over a certain hill called Milton, at the rising of the sun and the going down thereof, and the tentative fluttering talk of a girl who is destined to tread much in the lonely places of life and suffer much. Fortunately, there is there too the talk of a brave woman who sees life clearly and sees it whole, and whose verdict is, I am sure, that in spite of suffering and lonely places it is worth while.

I have not been able to get the edition of Keats's letters that I wanted you to see; I hope you will like the little picture which I send instead.

Faithfully yours,
WILLIAM VAUGHN MOODY.

To Daniel Gregory Mason

SUNDAY, Jan. 19, 1896.

DEAR DAN,

The news you send about your wrist is quite heart-breaking. I have not written sooner because I could not find it in my breast to speak comfort, feeling there only rebellion and disgust at the world order and its ghastly lack of breeding. How did you precipitate it? I can only fall back on thoughts of Schumann and his lame finger or whatever it was that spoiled him for concert gymnastics, and made him a minstrel in the court celestial. At any rate that question of composing away from the piano is settled, with a right parental emphasis from the slipper of Mischance. . . . I will spare you the usual admonition about the rigidity of your upper lip, in spite of the natural longing I feel to use the heirloom.

I have been brutally busy since getting back, on Uncle Horace's book,[1] so that all my schemes of spiritual conquest are done up in moth-balls for the time being. . . . One o'clock midnight, and the morrow flames responsibility. Hire a typewriter — marry one if necessary — and we will annihilate space. I have a creature to tell you about — but a Creature!

W. V. M.

[1] Some editorial work he had undertaken for Mr. Horace Scudder.

WILLIAM VAUGHN MOODY

To Daniel Gregory Mason

CHICAGO, Feb. 16, 1896.

DEAR DAN:

I have just heard from your sister-in-law of your enforced furlough. I am not going to help you curse your luck, knowing your native capabilities in that direction to be perfectly adequate, but my Methodist training urges me to give you an epistolary hand-grasp, the purport of which is "*Keep your sand.*" I could say other things, not utterly pharisaical. I could say what I have often said to myself, with a rather reedy tremolo perhaps, but swelling sometimes into a respectable diapason. "The dark cellar ripens the wine." And meanwhile, after one's eyes get used to the dirty light, and one's feet to the mildew, a cellar has its compensations. I have found beetles of the most interesting proclivities, mice altogether comradely and persuadable, and forgotten potatoes that sprouted toward the crack of sunshine with a wan maiden grace not seen above. I don't want to pose as resourceful, but I have seen what I have seen.

The metaphor is however happily inexact in your case, with Milton to retire to and Cambridge humming melodiously on the horizon. If you can only throttle your Daemon, or make him forego his leonine admonition "Accomplish," and roar you as any sucking dove the sweet vocable "Be," — you ought to live. I have got mine trained to that, pardee! and his voice grows not untunable. I pick up shreds of comfort out of this or that one of God's ashbarrels. Yesterday I was skating on a patch of ice in the park, under a poverty-stricken sky flying a pitiful rag of sunset. Some little muckers were guying a slim raw-boned Irish girl of fifteen, who circled and darted under their banter with complete unconcern. She was in the fledgling stage, all legs and arms, tall and adorably awkward, with a huge hat full of rusty feathers, thin skirts tucked up above spindling ankles, and a gay aplomb and swing in the body that was ravishing. We caught hands in midflight, and skated for an hour, almost alone and quite silent, while the rag of sunset rotted to pieces. I have had few sensations in life that I would exchange for the warmth of her hand through the ragged glove, and the pathetic curve of the half-formed breast where the back of my wrist touched her body. I came away mystically shaken and elate. It is thus the angels converse. She was something absolutely authentic, new, and inexpressible, something which only nature could mix for the heart's intoxication, a compound of ragamuffin, pal, mistress, nun, sister, harlequin, outcast, and bird of God, — with something else bafflingly suffused, something ridiculous and frail and savage and tender. With a world offering such rencontres, such aery strifes and adventures, who would not live a thousand years stone dumb? I would, for one — until my mood changes and I come to think on the shut lid and granite lip of him who has had done with sunsets and skating, and has turned away his face from all manner of Irish. I am supported by a conviction that at an auction on the steps of the great white Throne, I should bring more in the first mood than the second — by several harps and a stray dulcimer.

I thoroughly envy you your stay at Milton — wrist, Daemon, and all. You must send me a lengthy account of the state of things in Cambridge. . . . If the wrist forbids writing, employ a typewriter of the most fashionable tint — I will pay all expenses and stand the breakage. I stipulate that you shall avoid blondes however, they are fragile.

WILLIAM VAUGHN MOODY.

To Daniel Gregory Mason

CHICAGO, April 11, 1896.

MY DEAR DAN:

Yesterday morning mint appeared in the market windows, and this morning the lake is a swoon of silver and blue; — argal, I must write you a letter. I have felt for the past two weeks as if I had fallen heir to something, owing to the fact that spring turns out to be a month earlier here than in the east, and she comes over the prairies with the naïve confidence and sweet quick surrender that she has learned from the prairie girls. For the first time since your rustication I have ceased to envy you your domiciliation among the blue hills of Milton, for my side of the bubble has swung sunward and what care I if it be made of kitchen soap? I walk about in an amber clot of sensuousness, and feel the sap mount, like a tree. I thought — and often gloomily asseverated — that I had got over this purring rapture at the general situation, legitimately the gift of the primitive or the jagged. Well, I did not give Nature credit for the virtue that is in her.

My work, alas, still continues to be hard. I use up all my vital energies before the evening loaf

54

comes on, and then have force only for passive delights. I stick a good round straw into a cask of Spenser or Hardy, and suck myself to sleep — to dream of orchards and "golden-tongued Romance with serene lute." The hard bright sun of a western morning, with theme classes superimposed, reduces the golden tongue to phantom thinness of song and banishes the lute into the limbo of the ridiculous, but I plod on eveningwards with mole-like assiduity. I have come to realize the wonderful resources of passive enjoyment better than I ever did before — perhaps perversely, perhaps according to a mere instinct of self-preservation against the hurry and remorseless effectiveness of life out here. Whatever the cause, I have found out how good a thing it is to be a silly sheep and batten on the moor, to stand in cool shallows and let the water go by and the minnows dart and the brook moss stretch its delicate fingers. Also I seem to be coming, half through disappointed effort and half through this same effortlessness, to discern more clearly what is worthy in human motive and admirable in human achievement. It is not that I love Shakespeare less, but that I love Ophelia more.

W. V. M.

To Daniel Gregory Mason

MAY 16, 1896.

DEAR DAN:

Your letter came this morning in time to give me a goodly fit of the blues, thinking of Milton in spring, and thence by easy derivation of all the other excellencies from which my exiled feet are held. I can't repay the pang, but as the nearest thing to a heavenly affliction which I can command I send you a poem which I have just written about the Creature I once hinted to you of — a Girl who haunted the symphonies last winter. I hope you will like it, because it is almost the first thing I have done which has been a direct impulse from "real" life, and you know I have theories about that. Also what I tried to say is a thing which constitutes much of the poetry of a young man's life, I think, and if I could have got it said would have had a certain large interpretive value. Let me know your opinion, at as great length as your nerves and your nurse will permit.

WILL.

56

WILLIAM VAUGHN MOODY

WILDING FLOWER

TONIGHT her lids shall lift again
Slow-soft with vague desire,
And lay about my breast and brain
Their hush of lilac fire,
And I shall take the sweet of pain
As the laborer his hire.

And while the happy viols shake,
Under the paltry roof,
The web of singing worlds they make
To shelter Heaven aloof,
Our listening hearts shall build and break
Love's sempiternal woof.

O! listening heart, with all thy powers
Of white beatitude,
What is the dearest of God's dowers
To the children of his blood?
Where blow the lovesome wilding flowers
In the hollows of his wood?

That, though her ear hath never caught
The name men call me by,

That, though my lot from her sweet lot
Lyeth as sky from sky,
And my fain lonely hand dare not
Touch hers for comradery, —

Yet her shy devious lambent soul
With my slow soul should walk,
That linked like lovers we should stroll
By rivers of glad talk,
Or bow to the music's wind-control
As stalk by the lily stalk;

Yet never break, with a fool's mean waste,
The bubble of dream sky,
All gorgeous runnelled, window-spaced,
With blaze of drifted dye, —
This is a happiness to taste
Life's farthest meanings by.

The flushed adventurous violins
Climbing the crudded mist,
The clear horn calling when it wins
Its tower noon-precipiced,
The aching oboe throat that twins
Night's moonward melodist,

Shall find naught in the heavens of air
That they may name beside
The rhythmic joyance she doth wear
Whether she go or bide,
The wood-pool lustres of her hair,
Or her lip's wistful pride.

Oath-graven and heart-historied
Shall be our marriage ring,
Though oath of dead to sheeted dead
Be a louder spoken thing;
My sign shall be upon her head
While stars do meet and sing.

Not such a sign as women wear
Who bow beneath the shame
Of marriage insolence, and bear
A house-wife's faded name;
Nor such as passion eateth bare
With its carcanet of flame;

Nor such a sign as happy friend
Sets on his friend's dear brow,
When meadow pipings break and blend
To a key of subtle woe,
And the orchard says play-time's at end,
Best unclasp hands and go.

But where she strays, in blight or blooth,
One fadeless flower she wears,
A mystic gift God gave my youth,
Whose petals dim are fears,
Awes, adorations, songs of ruth,
Hesitancies and tears.

O! heart of mine, with all thy powers,
Of strange beatitude,
What is the dearest of God's dowers
To the children of His blood?
Where blow the lovesome wilding flowers
In the hollows of His wood?

WILLIAM VAUGHN MOODY.

May, 1896.

The revised form of this poem, printed in the "Poems" of 1901, is as follows: —

HEART'S WILD FLOWER

TO-NIGHT her lids shall lift again, slow, soft, with
vague desire,
And lay about my breast and brain their hush of spirit
fire,
And I shall take the sweet of pain as the laborer his
hire.

And though no word shall e'er be said to ease the
　　ghostly sting,
And though our hearts, unhoused, unfed, must still
　　go wandering,
My sign is set upon her head while stars do meet and sing.

Not such a sign as women wear who make their fore-
　　heads tame
With life's long tolerance, and bear love's sweetest,
　　humblest name,
Nor such as passion eateth bare with its crown of
　　tears and flame.

Nor such a sign as happy friend sets on his friend's
　　dear brow
When meadow-pipings break and blend to a key of
　　autumn woe,
And the woodland says playtime's at end, best unclasp
　　hands and go.

But where she strays, through blight or blooth, one
　　fadeless flower she wears,
A little gift God gave my youth, — whose petals dim
　　were fears,
Awes, adorations, songs of ruth, hesitancies, and tears.

O heart of mine, with all thy powers of white beatitude,
What are the dearest of God's dowers to the children
　　of his blood?
How blow the shy, shy wilding flowers in the hollows
　　of his wood!

To Daniel Gregory Mason

MAY 24, 1896.

DEAR DAN:

Thanks for your painstaking and very percep-
tive criticism. I cannot bring myself yet to accept
all your strictures unconditionally, but I find them
all suggestively and wisely hortatory, pointing the
way where the real pitfalls lie for me; and I know
that by the time I come to put the verses in permanent form I shall have accepted most of them
literally. Still, while I am still unpersuaded, let
me distinguish. The vague syntax of st. II is
undoubtedly mere slovenliness: the stanza shall
go the way of the ungirt loin. Also st. VII is as
you say turgid, and must go, even though it drag
with it the next stanza, which you like. As regards
the suspension of the sense in sts. IV–VI I cannot
agree. It seems to me that the breathlessness and
holding-aloof is justified by the emphasis with
which the concluding thought is thus given, and
still more by the fact that it sets the essential
thought off in a rounded form. It has a constructive value, also, as contrasting with the simple
declaratory forms of statement which precede
and follow it. I fancy it corresponds in my mind

somewhat to an "organ-point" in yours. The adjectives are too many, I know; but I am a little cold-blanketed and worried over your specific objections to phrase. "Paltry roof" is paltry, I freely admit; "wind-control" and "moonward melodist" are rococo as hell. But the other three to which you take exception I am sure are good poetry. . . . I think — pardon the egotism of the utterance (you would if you knew what tears of failure have gone to water the obstreperous little plant) — I think you are not tolerant enough of the instinct for conquest in language, the attempt to push out its boundaries, to win for it continually some new swiftness, some rare compression, to distill from it a more opaline drop. Is n't it possible, too, to be pedantic in the demand for simplicity? It's a cry which, if I notice aright, nature has a jaunty way of disregarding. Command a rosebush in the stress of June to purge itself; coerce a convolvulus out of the paths of catachresis. Amen!

W. V. M.

Please be good-natured and talk back. Or no, don't. Spare the arm.

To Daniel Gregory Mason

[CHICAGO,
June 23, 1896.]

DEAR DAN:

The report which you make of your lack of progress in health casts a gloom over my days. I am about starting for Wisconsin for a week's bicycling, and the monstrous egoism of bodily vigor which I feel, possesses my soul with shame. The thing for you to do is to come to Chicago: it is the greatest health resort going — *mirabile dictu*. We live on bicycling, base-ball, breezes, beer, and buncombe, and keep right chipper mostly. Can't you come out for a while? We have an extra bed-room, and if you can stand bachelor shiftlessness after the golden calm of Milton housekeeping, we could put you up "snugly." The quotation marks are only a warning as to the point of view. Expense need be no deterrent. Walking is good all the way, and hand-outs rich and plentiful. Think of it seriously. We will send you back *mens sana* surely and *sano corpore* if we have luck. Allons!

I have grown quite meek over the verses, as I thought I should. I accept your strictures on the suspended construction, with only the lingering spiteful affirmation that two persons to whom I read the poem seemed to find far less difficulty in following the syntax than you assert as normal. The alternative explanations of the discrepancy in judgment are both too disagreeable to pursue. At worst it is only one more failure; success only looms a little haughtier, a little more disdainful of conquest. Esperance and set on!

I have had an enormous little adventure since I wrote last. Another Girl, of course. This time a Westerner *par excellence* — a Californian, dating mentally from the age of Rousseau and Chateaubriand, with geysers and cloud bursts of romanticism, not to say sentimentality; dating spiritually from the Age of Gold, or some remoter purity, some Promethean dawn, some first foam-birth in hyperborean seas. She likes Gibson's drawings, adores Munsey's, and sings "Don't be Cross, Dear" with awful unction. After this you will not believe me when I say that she gave me the most unbearable shiver of rapture at the recognition of essential girlhood that I for a long time remember. Well, have you ever slept under the same roof with such a person, in the country, and wakened at that moment before dawn when in the "spectral uncompounded light" the spirit is least capable of defense, when it feels only a membrane separating it from the shock of joy and woe as they stream from the passionate day-spring, and have you felt the sense of that common shelter like a caress, heard through walls and doors the rise and fall of her breast as an ineffable rhythm swaying the sun? If you have you can realize the gone feeling that possessed me when she said (interpreting my own gloomy guess) that my kind was not her kind, that my language was not her language, and that her soul could only be studious to avoid mine, as the bird flying southward in spring avoids the hunter. I bowed assent and came home. I now nurse memories and grow elegiac. Come to Chicago!

W. V. M.

To Robert Morss Lovett

CHICAGO,
July 14, '96.

·   ·   ·   ·   ·   ·   ·

T—— turned up bright and early for his fifteen dollars, and continues to pay us little friendly visits from time to time. He now has his eye on the Civil Service. The Civil Service has not yet got its eye on him, but may in the fullness of time. . . .

It has been unspeakably hot — life a tragedy and a tongue-lolling — flat 7 a place of penance, teaching a Dantesque farce. Pray for us, thou godless happy Loafer.

Please give my kindest regards to Ida. I have for many weeks had it in my mind to try to phrase my gratitude for her very bully tolerance of our loudnesses and other iniquities this winter. Some day I shall, believe me; I speak with the arrogance of the professional rhetorician in daily need of defence against an inner conviction that he is the dumbest of God's creatures.

W. V. M.

To Josephine Preston Peabody

CHICAGO, July 17, 1896.

. . . .

I find that the West cries out as with one voice for the feathers and furbelows of feeling that you Cambridge mode-makers consigned to the garret decades ago. They're a little bedraggled at times, but we wear them with an air! Rousseau would weep over us — Chateaubriand would call us brother. I wonder if Rousseau and Chateaubriand were as ridiculous after all as they seem from the serene middle of Harvard Square?

All this is of course (I mean this sentimentalizing and toy-sea-sailing) by way of "compelling incident." That is the most illuminating and fruitful phrase you ever gave me. Every hour that I pilfer from tedium I thank the lips that framed it. Alas! the better ways of gilding the grey days slip from me. Apollo has gone a-hunting and I was n't asked. I have hung my harp on a willow, where it gathers rust and caterpillars with a zeal it lacked in a better cause. I am gone stark dumb. I rap myself and get a sound of cracked clay. A white rage seizes me at times, against the pottering drudgery that has fastened its lichen teeth on me and is softening down my "crisp cut name and date." I echo poor Keats's cry "O for ten years that I may steep myself in poetry" — with the modest substitution of weeks for years, and a willingness to compromise on as many days if Providence will only undertake to get this shiny taste of themes and literary drool out of my mouth, and let me taste the waters of life where they are near the well-head. To go a-brook-following — O happiness, O thou bright Denied!   W. V. M.

WILLIAM VAUGHN MOODY

To Daniel Gregory Mason

[CHICAGO,
July 20, 1896.]

DEAR DAN:

The confident tone of your last letter puts me in conceit with life again. Envisage the theme job with the comic or the tragic mask, as you please, but not with the features sweet Nature gave you — on your life. I am known in the Chicago themery as the Man in the Iron Mask, and you may wager I live up to the title. The chance of luring you out here in August tempts me to lie goldenly about the musical prospects. Now that I have the strength I hasten feebly to falter that they are damn poor. Not that Chicago is not "musical" — it is amazingly and egregiously so. Calliope is the one Muse we recognize, and she has a front spare bedroom and unlimited pie. But the place is overrun with music teachers — chiefly foreign — whereof I find recorded the names of unbelievable thousands. The University does not yet boast a Department of Music, though one hears rumors of millions ripe to drop at the summons of One Elect. If you feel the star quite distinct above your brows, you might practice crooking your little finger with the proper imperial persuasion.

You don't tell me anything about people. I have become a frowsy gossip, and cannot live without my pill of personalities sweetly compounded. To punish you for the neglect I enclose a reaction on a recent notable Experience. Hire an amanuensis for seven hours and talk out a sufficing bundle of pages on the mystical differences between This and That, and send the bill along with the bundle.

WILL.

P.S. Before reading my poor little reaction, do me the justice to abstract yourself for twelve hours from the society of ——, — to whom, by the way, I send my warmest regards. I have just enjoyed his article in the Chap Book.

The "reaction on a recent notable Experience" here referred to was rejected by Moody when he came to make up the "Poems" of 1901 — for what reason is not very evident. Mrs. Moody says that he felt that "The Golden Journey" made it superfluous. The style of the two poems is doubtless somewhat similar, but "Dawn Parley" has a simple directness and a poignancy that the other lacks. At any rate there can be no harm in reprinting it here as an excellent example of its author's earlier manner.

WILLIAM VAUGHN MOODY

DAWN PARLEY

I WOKE upon the edge of day,
The east was wild with racing light,
All meek and wild my spirit lay
Star-shaken with delight.

I said, "This moment she doth wake
Within the chamber next but one,
She sees the morning-glory shake
Its trumpets to the sun."

A bird that had his headstrong say
Outside my casement, frilled and went;
All wild and wan my spirit lay
With sudden anguish rent.

For yesternight I laid my brain
And all my soul's dim banded powers
Open to her, who said, "'T is plain
Thy ways are none of ours."

"Though nobly good to thine and thee,
To us thy ways are strange and drear;
I go with my sweet friends to be,
And thou must tarry here."

71

Above the hurry of the light
All meek and wild my spirit hung,
From the far hills I scared the night
And in the zenith sung,

"O! playmates of her heedless hours,
Her eyes ye nevermore may see:
My brain and all my soul's dim powers
Possess her utterly."

W. V. M.

July 18, 1896.

To Mrs. C. H. Toy

[CHICAGO, August 11, 1896.]

As for Chicago, I find that it gives me days or at least hours of broad-gauge Whitmanesque enthusiasm, meagerly sprinkled over weeks of tedium. The tedium is not of the acid-bath sort, however. Genuinely, I feel mellower, deeper-lunged, more of a lover of life, than I have ever felt before, and the reason is that I have had long somnolent spaces in which to feel the alchemy of rest. I am writing, not much, but with time enough to listen for the fairy echoes, to turn and taste again, to fix and prefer. I shall never have a lordly shelf-full of books to point to ("Paint my two hundred pictures, some good son!") but if I live out the reasonable span, I think I can hope to have one little one at least, or two maybe, which will be in their own way *vocal* from cover to cover. Whether the voice will be one that people will care to hear, matters less to me than it did — perhaps less than it should. Safely stowed in my gum-cell, with my globule of amber honey, I find it easy to forget Leviathan and his egregious spoutings. He begins to seem the least bit comical, Leviathan, from the gum-cell outlook. The fact that we and our cell could hang unobserved on one of his eyelashes, does n't negate our importance in the least. . . .

To Robert Morss Lovett

CHICAGO, August 16, 1896.

DEAR ROB:

. . . .

The Morgenthau message was, as you with characteristic charity surmise, of friendly import. It is only natural that the terse impassioned utterance of great minds under stress, should have floored the telegraph operator. Hard luck that your summer should have got away from you with so little to show in the way of essentials —

by which I do not need to say I mean alluvial soaks and happy drools, rather than land travel and seafaring.

Chicago has been a woe and a bitterness this summer. Both Ferd and I hate the shop and all it contains with a physical hatred. We are looking for the man who said the summer was cool and a good time to work. . . .

To Daniel Gregory Mason

[CHICAGO,
August 27, 1896.]

DEAR DAN:

So far from considering your letter "merely silly" I found it really stirring — at least after I got over my amusement, which you must grant to the weakness of the flesh. The chief reason why I have not replied sooner is (prepare to be shocked beyond speech) that I have been trying to make up my mind which side has the least injustice and unwisdom to its account in this matter. Living here in the heart of the debtor's country I have come to see that the present regime cannot possibly endure. Free silver is undoubtedly a desperate remedy — perhaps an insane one; but the slow asphyxiation which the vast farming population of the West is undergoing from the appreciation of deferred payments on their gigantic mortgage debt, due to the inadequacy of the maximum gold coinage to keep pace with the growth of values — calls for immediate relief of some sort. I have seriously thought, had indeed before you wrote seriously thought, of doing a little stumping during the fall vacation, but on which side my voice and vote will fall is still a matter of debate with me. This is the utmost abyss and downward of my recreancy.

I envy you your feverish and on-the-whole delightful visitings with a poisonous tin-green envy. I have about got my mouth full of western heartiness and uniplexity, and long for the lands of purple haze and wicked goat-shanks of apothegm footing it after the shy fluttered robes of dryad metaphor. Abbott Thayer must be a daisy: tell me about him. O to walk in a far sweeter country, among dim many-colored bushes! O now to drink a brown drop of happiness with my good friend! Selah!

I note with grief the catalogue of black-prowed ships the Gods have winged with disaster against your spirit's Troy. Anxious counting will not seem to make them fewer. I would urge you again to brave the blustering rigors of the west, if it did not seem such abandoned selfishness to do so. For me to go East now would not only be to "break a trace," but to break for a hasty feast the little pot of honey I have stored up by much noon-day toil to serve for a long long starveling joy next summer and the winter after. I shall only be able to pull through the winter on the prospect of nine months of golden liberty at the end — the epithet being, let me hasten to add, notably metaphorical.

The Singer refuses to comfort my exile with so much as a shed feather of song. My letters lie unanswered and my tear-bottles cumber the Dead-Letter Office. Wherefore are these thusly? Ah me, to walk in a country of dim many-colored bushes, beside bright-breathing waters! To hear the shy bird that woke at evening in the breast of my friend! Selah.

I was glad to hear you liked the Atlantic article. I am in a state of rawness and jealousy when praise of even a pot-boiler makes me lick the hand of the giver. Desperate is the pass of all little Gods who say after the sixth day, "This is my handi-work, and lo, it is mostly Lolly-pop!"

Divinely yours,   W. V. M.

WILLIAM VAUGHN MOODY

To Josephine Preston Peabody

AUGUST 30 [1896?].

Are n't you ever going to speak to me again?
Is my back-yard left irremediably desolate? Have
your rag dolls and your blue dishes said inexorable
adieu to my cellar-door? The once melodious
rain-barrel answers hollow and despairing to my
plaints — but for that the summer is mute.
What have I done? What have I left undone?
Alas, these questions are the ancient foolishness
of the Rejected. Forgive me that the rejected are
foolish, but tell me my sin. But a little while ago
you were my intercessor with one whom I had
inscrutably offended, and now you visit upon my
head inscrutable doom. Imagine the panic of a
spider who has anchored his web to the pillars of
the firmament and discovers of a sudden that they
are the spokes of a bicycle in active requisition.
Such a one so smote me yesterday with his alle-
gory that I plucked him, silky ruin and all, from
his fool's paradise, and deposited him among the
comfortable rafters. Will you be outdone in
charity? My web is a sight — and Messieurs the
flies, once my toothsome prey, beleaguer me,
buzzing annihilation.   W. V. M.

Categorically, I crave answer to the following questions: —

1. Where are you to be next year?
2. What are you going to do there?
3. Where have you been this summer?
4. What did you do there?
5. What are your latest *opera?* (a ms. copy of same should accompany reply.)
6. What are your contemplated opera? (May be omitted for cause.)
7. Are you happy?
8. Are you well?
9. Are you still friends?

N.B. Please answer the questions in the order given. Use only plain idiomatic English. You will be judged by both the quality and the quantity of your writing.

To Daniel Gregory Mason

CHICAGO,
November 24, 1896.

DEAR DAN:

So far from being able to "dartle a ray of poesy" into your world, I contrast the vivid glow of that world as set forth in your letter, with the kennel I inhabit, in a spirit of blank misgiving. Fourteen consecutive months of hack teaching[1] have left me in a state of spiritual beggary I never dreamed of, and the seven months that still roll their vermiform length before me sometimes startle me into a Bedlam query. The uncourageous truth must be told, that I have got already to the lees of my resisting power, and at the best can only crawl stricken and tolerated to the latter end. The spirit of selection, the zest of appropriation, is gone out of me. For a more instant misery, I must give up my Christmas trip east, to which my rheumy eyes have long been straining for light. A new course to read for, and a pinching poverty, are the main reagents in this stinking bit of chemistry; at the black bottom of the retort lieth Little Willy's calcined pebble of a heart. Sing a song of willow. Strew on him sawdust, sawdust, with never a hint of goo. Convey a poor devil's plangent gratitude to your mother and your sister-in-law for their offered hospitality. This reminds me — how did Mrs. Milton Mason get it into her head that she had offended me? Let her know that in my present state, perhaps in any state, a snub or a cuffing from her likes would be unto me as rarest hydromel, since after

[1] That is, since October, 1895.

all even a snub or a cuffing constitutes a sort of bond. The blue beatitude of those Milton hills often yearns into the grey drift over Chicago roofs, and I hear thence, even in the midst of cable-car-gongs and elevator chains, a spectral hymnody. . . .

Your statement of your musical condition fills me with sorrow and wrath. Your letter reached me just as I was starting for the Friday afternoon Symphony rehearsal, and darkened for me this one flower of passion and color that still blooms where the city of my soul once was. But in the midst of a Schumann thing my eye wandered to the program and read there the story of his being turned by just such a misfortune as yours into the work which was so gloriously his to do. Of course you know the story, but I could hardly help sitting down at once and calling upon you, beseeching you to think of it again. For you to give up music for "letters" is for an oyster to renounce pearl-making in order to devote its energies to the composition of sea-weed pills. I hasten to add that this is n't saying a damn against the pills. . . .

W. V. M.

WILLIAM VAUGHN MOODY

To Mary L. Mason

CHICAGO.
Jan. 14, 1897.

MY DEAR MRS. MASON, —

Believe me, I was not nearly so unheedful of your Song of the Milton hills, as my silence has seemed to say. The two or three days which I spent at your house, with those hills for background, taught me their power of saying "Be still and know." Those few days stand out with a singular lustre — no, that is hardly the word — with a quality, a *timbre*, which often surprises me with its recurrence and residence. Please don't suspect me of "registering sensations," but this mysterious wilfulness of the memory in aggrandizing this experience and annulling that, out of all reason and proportion so far as one can judge from the outside, often sets me wondering who is boss of me, anyhow. Whoever he is, in this particular instance I submit cheerfully to his dictum.

As Dan may have told you I have been living a rather shrouded existence of late, owing to many circumstances which are hardly worth retailing one by one, but which in the mass make up a very respectable incubus. My term of dur-

81

ance in the academic stocks, however, has been sensibly shortened: I expect to get on to Boston before the end of April, to meet some of God's people once more before setting out for God's country. Isn't it singular that really good humans all seem like *emigrés*, trying bravely but rather forlornly to persuade themselves that the land of their adoption is the land of Heart's Desire? By which sapient query you can gauge the state of my nervous reservoirs: a whining sentimentality such as that can only be excused or accounted for by the nigh yawning of the ineloquent tomb.

I will not try to thank you for your multiplied kindnesses, of which your letter was not the least.

Always earnestly yours,

WILLIAM VAUGHN MOODY.

To Daniel Gregory Mason

[CHICAGO,
Feb. 23, 1897.]

DEAR DAN:

Your letter arouses my conscience from the daze into which I some months ago drugged and sand-bagged it in order that it might not interfere with the performance of meaner but more pressing duties than the ones it clamored of. I have treated my friends shamefully, though every day I see more clearly that they are the principal thing, and that without them, or at least without the sense of them in the background, life would be but, as we are informed on good authority it is, a Vale of Tears. I have been rather ashamed to write for one thing, for fear of revealing my barrenness, but if one hath only a clout to his breech should he therefore hide him forever in a dog-hutch? Thus spake Zarathustra. This quarter I have been held down to business with particular attentiveness on the part of the divine chastener of my spirit: besides my theme work I have been giving a course in the seventeenth century poets, reading in them all night and writing lectures on them all day. Good fun, and I have made some rare finds — of which expect to hear more anon — but rather hard on one's tire. I hasten to assure you that I am as yet unpunctured, though much worn at the rim, and rapidly losing resiliency through leakage. I relinquish the figure with reluctance. . . .

I can't tell yet whether I shall get on to Boston before sailing. I fear not, as I can get very cheap rates east on the Baltimore and Ohio, and my steamer (Anchor Line to Naples) is apt to up and sail any old day after I get away from here, thus making the extra trip to Boston a very hurried one at best. Moreover, in my present tan-bark state of soul I should be as dull to you as I am to myself. In any case I shall stop for a week or ten days on my return in the fall, when I shall be trailing clouds of glory of the most diapered design, and when, moreover, the tennis will be ripe enough to pull, to say nothing of country walks and things.

. . . .

To Josephine Preston Peabody

HARVARD CLUB, 27 WEST 44th St.
March 26, 1897.

MY DEAR FRIEND:

Now that I have at last emerged from darkness *a riveder le stelle*, I turn to you as Dante to Casella, and beg at least a word to prove that Florence still has true hearts. I am still rather numb as to brain and drab-colored as to soul, but I can feel the holy influences that wait upon him who loafs beginning to purge me and urge me, though I tremble to say so for fear of frightening back their shy inquiring tentacles. The thought of six whole months of acquaintance with myself fills me with an inexpressible arrogance, the likes of which I did n't suspect my meek pedagogical make-up of. I had promised myself for a long time a few days tarry in Boston before sailing, but got caught as usual between the contracting prongs of time and space. So, instead of the long afternoon or afternoons during which I had hoped to rummage the past and peer into the future with you, here I am with a half-hour and a sheet of paper. Nevertheless, that will suffice for the cardinal question — How is it with you? What is the news from the Niche? Won't you tell me, through the medium of Messrs. Whitby and Co., 5 Via Tornabuoni, Florence?

W. V. M.

During the six months' trip to Italy and the Austrian Tyrol that Moody now made, he wrote "Good Friday Night" and the "Road Hymn for the Start," and began work on the "Masque of Judgment." He returned to Chicago in September, 1897, and undertook, in addition to his teaching, at the suggestion of Mr. Horace E. Scudder, whom he refers to as "Uncle Horace," the editing of the Cambridge Edition of Milton's Poetical Works.

To Ferdinand Schevill

CASA FROLLO, GIUDECCA.
VENICE, June 8th, '97.

DEAR FERD:

I have put off writing to you from day to day, partly by reason of the manifold demands which Venice makes on one's powers of sensation and utterance, but principally by reason of the delay which my intimate connections with the patrician houses of Milan failed to prevent in the forwarding of my negatives. Here they are at last, such ones as I have got printed: rejoice over them duly.

I have been installed in the Casa Frollo with the Lovett family for two weeks, and many blessings have been showered upon us. Foremost to be mentioned among Heaven's gifts is a garden, green and voiceful, reaching back through checkered vistas to the Lagoon — a regularly bang-up place of dalliance. Lacketh as yet a laughing Lalage; as yet, I repeat, not without a sinking at the heart. Meanwhile Euterpe floats at the ends of the vineyard alleys, elusive, promising. The Good-Friday theme has taken shape;

3.

More silently than new-found friends,
To whom much silence makes amends
In the much babble vain
While yet their lives were twain,

We walked along the odorous hill.

His figure ashen-stoled
Scale in the moon's broad gold.

=

William Vaughn Moody

Norwich: April '77.

it proved more modest in scope in the working out than I had anticipated, but I am almost satisfied with it nevertheless. I hope you may not frown upon it, when in the fullness of time it is chanted before you. I am at work now on a rather hopelessly fantastic thing, I fear, half-lyric, half-dramatic; I shall try to excuse the wilfulness of the form by calling it a Masque. The subject is the Judgment-day — no less — a kind of sketchy modern working over of the theme, from the point of view of the accusing human. God Almighty promises to be an engaging figure, with proper foreshortening. The protagonist is the archangel Raphael, a staunch humanist (his enemies — Heaven confound their counsels! — would say a sentimentalist), and principal rôles are sustained by such pleasing characters as the Seventh Lamp of the Throne, the Angel of the Pale Horse, the Lion of the Throne, and the Spirit of the Morning-star. I foresee great possibilities, — a kind of Hebrew Götterdämmerung, with a chance for some real speaking-out-in-meeting — hoop-la! — Excuse my barbaric yawp; it is merely meant to express enthusiasm.

We keep a gondola-slave, and make frequent trips to the Lido, which however is dull as yet.

The weather grows hot and heavy apace; I fear we shall have to make a break for the mountains before long.

. . . .

W. V. M.

To Josephine Preston Peabody

CORTINA D'AMPEZZO,
TYROL, July 15, 1897.

MY DEAR MISS JOSEPHINE PRESTON PEABODY:
I have not answered your unfriendly and inadequate letter sooner because I found myself incapable of mustering the amount of ill-feeling which I judged commensurate with the demands of a reply. I have, indeed, given up all hope of such a strenuous accession, and have resolved merely to hide the fountains of my good will under a decent covering of recrimination, throwing my human longing for retaliation to the winds. I am the more moved to measures of pacification because, in the first place, my return to New England shores has grown suddenly more imminent, and in the second, because I hear news of noble Works taking shape and soul under your hands. It is now nearly three weeks since I fled here to this sky-hung, cloud-acquainted village of the Austrian

Tyrol from the too generous ardors of an Italian summer. I am moved to harrow your literary sensibilities with "description" of these wind-swept valley pastures, hedged in by ferocious peaks, and dowered, even to the border of the snow, with unimaginable wealth of wild bloom. Tremble not, I will not maltreat a captive of courtesy. To tell the ignoble truth, as my time of liberty draws to an end, and I see how very little I have accomplished in it, I find myself trying to shut out sensations which are too poignant and crowding, in order that I may find the restfulness necessary for work. I have arrived at a depth of miserliness where it is possible for me to give up a night in the star-lit grass for a night of lamp-oil and muddy ink. Not that I have done much, or shall, I fear; but I have a good thing to do, when it pleases Apollo. I have just had a letter from Uncle Horace, making propositions — messes of pottage: it is the reek and fatness thereof which draws my Esau-soul homeward before its appointed time — perhaps.

W. V. M.

'Address, care Whitby and Co.
5 Via Tornabuoni, Florence.

To Daniel Gregory Mason

ALBERGO D'ESPAGNA, VIA CALZAIOLI,
FLORENCE, August 1, 1897.

DEAR DAN:

When I found in the batch of letters awaiting me here this morning one from you, remorse, long dozing, awoke and gnawed. I have been a monster of taciturnity and greedy possession; I have lain on my gorgeous heap of sensation like Fafnir on the Glittering Hoard, growling from my *papier-maché* throat to all importunate duties and memories, "Lass mich fühlen! Ich lieg und besitze." As I count over my rosary of Italian days — and nights! — with the little seed pearls and the pearls of price and the green gawdies, a sense of profound pity for everybody else in the world invades my breast, — now at least when the imminent prospect of a return to the key of drab sends over me a sense of moral realities once more. The substance of your letter as well as its tone precipitates this floating compassion about yourself, a reaction of the spiritual chemistry for which you will doubtless thank me as little as I should you in a reversed case. That your arm does not pick up, that ——'s beard has again been

known to stick out straight, that —— laughs a
hyena laugh before relapsing into ambrosial
silence, to say nothing of your estrangement from
the mint julep and its realms of gold — all together constitute a desolating picture — so desolating indeed that I hesitate to communicate a
plan I had formed for spending the month of
September in Boston. The only scrap of comfort
I get, fortunately an intensive one, is the paren-
thetical assurance that you spend the hoarded
strength of your arm in writing music. I have
never quite got over the shock given me by your
announcement six months ago that music was
not for you. There seemed something obscene
about such a blow to your chance of happiness,
such a lopping off. I remember once seeing a play-
mate coming out of his door on crutches after he
had lost a foot. Bah! my soul sickens yet, after
fifteen years. These things should not be done
after these ways. My golden bath, my Semele-
shower of sensation, has only strengthened my
conviction that the adventures of the mind are
beyond all compare more enthralling than the
adventures of the senses, that no twining of
amorous limbs can bring the intoxication of the
airy grappling of the Will to Beauty with the

feminine latency of thought toward being beautifully created upon. I hope that is not as snarled as it looks on paper, though I know it's full as bawdy.

This conviction is perhaps the best thing I have to show for my vacation, however. I observe with sudden retrospective dismay that I have accomplished next to nothing in printable pages, one or two short poems, and a couple of torsoes sketched out in the block, but so big that my mallet and chisel lose themselves in the interstices between dust speck and dust speck. I clamber with Liliputian ingenuity over the bulk thereof, spying out, very agile and bustling, with horny eye apprehensive upon cracks and precipices. As yet no planet-displacing news.

Remains to be communicated my plan for September: this: Uncle Horace has had the *gentilezza* to offer me a substantial job of book-editing, which if I accomplish in due season will insure me another playing-space months earlier than I could otherwise hope for it. I propose accordingly to cut short off here, sail on the 19th August for America, reach Boston by the first of September, and spend the ensuing four weeks working in the Boston and Cambridge libraries, with seasons of torso-climbing and mint-juleping generously interspersed

Till when —

WILL.

P.S. When you write abroad again use tissue-paper and invisible ink and write on both sides. My disbursements to the Italian government and the Postal Union on your blue-book amounted to just eighty-five (85) centesimi. Not that it was n't worth ninety (90), but thrift is thrift.

W. V. M.

To Daniel Gregory Mason

5488 EAST END AVENUE,
CHICAGO.
[January 3, 1898.]

DEAR DAN:

My gratitude for your stout refusal to forget my existence at last forces me to open my lips in some galvanic sign of sentience. Having got them unlocked I can do little more than let them gape, for I have quite lost the use and want of speech — at least civilized speech. I have mastered the local symbols of communication and can now carry on conversation of some length with the native population, but it has been at the expense of my English. I counted my vocabulary last night and discovered it to consist of ninety - three words. You shall have them all, if you will promise not to be reckless with them.

. . . I am unable at present to express my emotion over your propaganda of my fame, in a more robust way than by enclosing the Good Friday Night. Jetsam I have n't a decent copy of, nor time to make one. I started in today on another quarter's work at the shop — with vacation and restored consciousness three months away. From now until April I shall not have time to say a Credo; but when the spring is in the air you may look for me to drop down on you out of the first blue sky. . . . Of "spiritual encounters" I have had — am having — one; but it is too solemn to talk about, short of midnight and the third glass — if then. . . . This is a sneaking poor return for your good letters, but I am dead tired and tomorrow is wash-day.

WILL.

WILLIAM VAUGHN MOODY

To Josephine Preston Peabody

CHICAGO.
Jan. 5, 1898.

I have just been telling Dan that the alms of remembrance which my Cambridge friends (the term is inclusive) still bestow at feast-time upon me, are taken with no less gratitude because the lockjaw which prevents me from nourishing my leanness with them also somewhat impedes my speech. As for the new year you point a hortatory finger at — *speriamo!* April is only eighty-eight lectures, forty committee meetings and several thousand themes away, and then I shall be for a little time my own man again, with a chance to look about and say "Well!" Whether it is to be an expletive rather than a considering adverb, the gods and several little people have on their knees. . . .

W. V. M.

To Robert Morss Lovett

5488 EAST END AVE.,
CHICAGO, Feb. 21, 1898.

DEAR ROB:
Your letter and the pictures bring home to me my epistolary shortcomings with a painful dis-

tinctness. I blush with shame when I reflect that a scribbled postcard from Viareggio, which you probably never got, is the only sign of remembrance and gratitude I have made since our good times at Cortina and thereabouts. But to my heart my heart was voluble.

Thanks for the pictures; they fall cool and lovely on an eye grown horny with animadversive gazing upon Chicago art and nature. I find to my considerable depression that Chicago does not subdue me to her graces any more masterfully than she did two years ago. Indeed, these last six months have made me almost as fanatically homesick for civilization as my former seven quarters succeeded in doing. I lay it, stoutly, to a higher organization of the sensorium, but I inwardly suspect that it is owing to a depleted sand. In either case, release is at hand; I leave in less than a month for New York. I should have let you know ere this that Spain is out of the question for me this year. In the first place I have n't the cash, in the second, my Milton is not yet completed, and in the third, the climacteric, I want to get a little volume of verse ready for press before fall at latest. The Masque, of which you make friendly inquiry, is so far as concretions go, much where Cortina left it; but I have thought about it a good deal, and believe I can jam it through, with a little leisure. Why do you treat the novel with such novercal rigor? By all means put it out, before you come back and assume all the stifling dignities that await you.

. . . .

Remember me to Stickney. I read some of his mss. the other day, sent me by Savage. He has certainly strengthened much, but does n't seem to have quite achieved yet the synthesis of Browning with Verlaine, at which he manifestly aims.

With warmest regards for Ida and the Bambini (O egregious plural!) and felicitations upon your own patriarchal head, and sorrowings of spirit over lost Andalusia,

As ever,   WILL.

The following letter is undated, but as Mrs. Marks published her first book, "The Wayfarers," in 1898, it may from the internal evidence be assigned to the early months of that year.

To Josephine Preston Peabody

Thanks for the good tidings; they have shed about me a reflected glow of spiritual *bien-être* rare enough in the procession of my days to be relished,

I tell you. Then it was n't all reflected either, nor will it altogether go with the fading of the ink. It is jolly that some of us are going to have a say; the elected one must be spokesman for the rejected, and say it with an air and a gesture! Not without responsibility, in view of the others, listening glad but a little jealous, hoping to hear it put just their way, and ready to lift protesting hands if it is n't. I could swallow my own little hiccough of envy with a better grace if I were there to dogmatize over title and title-page, order and grouping and pruning and padding. I suppose you will have to struggle along your unillumined way without me, poor thing; but there will come a day of reckoning for all shortcomings, when I crawl over your pages, horny eye animadversive upon this and that, antennae excitedly waving. And if all is good and seemly without and within, I shall go away mollified, and there shall be no more drudging that day but only joy, in the kingdom of Ants.

The jewelled white of the New England winter! Here it is mud — sky, lake, boulevard, factory, flat, one featureless contiguity of Mud — to say nothing of People and their Insides.

W. V. M.

WILLIAM VAUGHN MOODY

To Daniel Gregory Mason

CHICAGO,
March 13, 1898.

DEAR DAN:

. . . Thanks for Dunn's poem: I found it delightfully rapt and Keatsian: its vagueness is not annoying, for it is the vagueness of youth. (I wish you could see a picture I have over my desk at this moment — an Antonelli da Messina — a boy's face full of mystical yearning, set in a background of dim trees.) Apropos of verses, the Atlantic has taken my Good Friday Night. The Bard [Miss Peabody] tells me, with "valorous" tears, that Copeland refuses to put out her book before fall, which I suppose is preliminary to the crawl direct. *Sunt lachrymae rerum.*

. . . .

About April 1, Moody arrived in New York and took a room at 109 Waverley Place. He was working hard on his edition of Milton, but also found time to write out the "Masque of Judgment" in somewhat tentative and fragmentary form. This he read to me in Boston, early in June. He returned to Chicago for the summer and autumn quarters' teaching, spent the Christmas holidays in Boston, and in the first days of 1899 established himself in New York again, this time at 318 West 57th St.

To Daniel Gregory Mason

"THE PLAYERS."
NEW YORK, April 8, 1898.

DEAR DAN:

. . . The plan you outline for the Easter vacation is so tempting that if you had sprung it on me soon enough I suppose I should have yielded to your blandishments and given New York the go-by. Once here, however, I feel that I ought to stay. If I mistake not, my lines are apt to be cast in these places permanently in the not distant future, and I have a good chance now to make some acquaintances and learn the ropes of New York life against that desirable time. I have already met a number of capital chaps here at the Players, where Carpenter has kindly set me down — chiefly playwrights, not very big ones I suspect, but full of enthusiasm and practical expedient. The great thing about them is that they get their things played, and that sort of thing, begad, begins to appeal to me. Do not believe me quite recreant to ideals; Cambridge and her elegiac air seems still lovely and of good report. But these chaps here, though very moderately elegiac and of a dubious report, are splendidly American and contemporary; and I feel convinced that this is the place for young Americans who want to do something. (N.B. *I have not enlisted in the marine.*)

. . . As for yourself, go to Chocorua by all means, and believe me with you in wistful imagination when the spring sun gilds your mountain tops and absorbs the spare goo from my asphalt pavements.

As ever

W. V. M.

To Daniel Gregory Mason

THE PLAYERS.

April 13, 1898.

DEAR DAN:

. . . Thanks for the addresses: I shall certainly look up Harry. If you know any other good people here, send me their names and whereabouts and a card of introduction. I am going in for people now, having made the discovery that the average man is among the most unexpected and absorbing of beings. . . .

[To Ferdinand Schevill.]

THE PLAYERS.
16 GRAMERCY PARK.
Easter Sunday —'98.

DEAR FERD:

I was sorry not to see you to say goodbye, though the weeks that intervene between now and July 1st, when the summoning hour calls me to penance, are already shortening so visibly that the ceremony of leave-taking seems superfluous. New York I find all I fondly imagined, and more. The fellows I have met here are immensely cordial; they have set me down at two or three interesting clubs where I am gradually getting an insight into this wonderfully virile and variegated life. Here at the Players especially there are no end of beguiling humans. Most of them are only moderately elegiac, to be sure, and their allegiance to the sisters of the sacred well is tempered by their interest in the genie of the box-office till; but they are splendidly American and contemporary, and some of them are doing good work. I dined last night with the man who did Tess over, and the air of getting things jammed through which pervaded him is pleasantly characteristic

102

of the whole crowd. Whatever the young American art-producer is, as I see him here in his essence, he is certainly not lily-livered. The generalization is inspiriting.

Milton is stalking along with his usual austerity toward completing himself, and besides I get a little time for better things. . . .

W. V. M.

To Daniel Gregory Mason

CHICAGO, Dec. 2, 1898.

DEAR DAN:

This is an attempt to forestall your righteous wrath at my ungentlemanly neglect of your letters, which have been meat and drink to me at the seasons of their arrival and for long after. I will accept any punishment except a refusal on your part to rejoice over the fact that I am coming to Cambridge for Christmas week. Intend thy thoughts towards revelry, for there must be mad times. Like a sick and lonesome gilligalloo bird I begin to think on me native sugar-cane swamps, and plume me feathers for a flight thither where the carnivoristicous Philistine invadeth not with his pot-gun of Important Business, and neither moth nor dust doth corrupt. Don't tell me you aint going to be to home, for I'm acalculatin' on you for my main holt.

W. V. M.

To Mrs. C. H. Toy

CHICAGO, Dec. 5, 1898.

MY DEAR MRS. TOY:

This is to say that I expect to spend Christmas week in Cambridge. . . . I am eager for the queer inimitable charm of Cambridge, for that atmosphere of mind at once so impersonal and so warm, for that neatness and decency of you children who have been washed and dressed and sent to play on the front lawn of time by old auntie Ding-an-Sich, while we hoodlums contend with the goat for tomato cans in the alley. I have a fair line of the same to lay before your eyes when I am admitted inside the aristocratic front gate: some of them will make a fine effect in a ring around your geranium bed.

To Daniel Gregory Mason

[CHICAGO, Dec. 19, 1898.]

1. Arrive Friday P.M. or Saturday A.M. Exact time to be communicated later.

2. Will stay at 39 with pleasure.

3. Think Chocorua too risky, especially for your purposes of recuperation.

4. You shall loaf, sir.

5. You shall go to themes once more on Jan. 2 in a galliard, and conduct consultations in a coranto.

W. V. M.

To Josephine Preston Peabody

318 WEST 57th ST.
NEW YORK, Jan. 8, 1899.

MY DEAR FRIEND:

I put off writing Hail and Godspeed when the Book came out because I wanted to speak my words of pride and praise in person. You were not there to hear them, and since then I have been caught in the wheels of this world's business. But you cannot but believe me when I say that the book gave me a very keen delight, first because it was yours and second because it was the world's, and read in cold type it entirely justified my old enthusiasm. Some things, which seemed to me less mature and less forthright, I could have wished away; and others I could have wished a little nearer the every day speech: but even for these the *Envoi* made *amende honorable.*

105

What we expect of you now is to fulfill the promise there made: to take hold of the common experience and the common idiom and glorify it. Who am I, to be sure, that I should be offering sage advice? Yet I hope you ask the question without sarcasm, for after all I am one who has loved the Muses well, and hoped much from my friends, however I may seem to have forgotten both the one and the other.

W. V. M.

To Daniel Gregory Mason

HARVARD CLUB.
27 West 44th St.
Jan. 17, 1899.

DEAR DAN:

I certainly sha'n't let you off, now that you have been rash enough to make advances. 'F yez don' wan' the pants, w'y in hell 'd you try 'em on fur, blokey? I answer your questions categorically.

1. You can see all of me all of the time after and including lunch, which I usually take about 1.30; from the mysteries of my bath, breakfast, and matutinal galumphing o'er twin-peaked Parnassus, I shall exclude you peremptorily, but after 1.30 I am yours till cock-crow.

2. My luncheon, consisting of a sandwich and a drink, usually costs ten (10) cents, unless I frequent a free-lunch counter, when it costs five (5). Since looking at the expanse of cheek in the picture which you send (and for which I thank you kindly) I have about resolved to intermit lunches for the time being. If this sounds too Spartan, remember that a great deal of Nourishment can be bought between Washington Square and Central Park, if you still feel atrophied after lunching with me. For dinner I pay (including tip) from sixty to eighty-five cents, except on rare occasions when I feel proud and sassy — on which occasions I sometimes reach the dizzy and disastrous peak of a dollar ten.

3. The weather will be fine. Shut up, I say it *will!*

I have n't touched the Masque,[1] but have plunged *in medias res* with the play.[2] It bids fair to be short (perhaps 50 minutes to an hour to act) but it's developing pretty well. I found myself embarrassed a good deal at first by the dull monochromatic medium of everyday speech, but

[1] That is, since making the first draft the preceding spring.
[2] The first draft of what eventually became "The Faith Healer."

am getting more used to it now and find that when you do get an effect in it it is more flooring than anything to be got with bright pigments. I am trying hard to give it scenic structure, for as I conceive it nearly half of it will be dumb show; at least a great deal of its effectiveness will depend on the acting. I shall have it ready to read to you — at least in first draft — when you appear. I've got a Chinese restaurant to show you on Mott Street; likewise a Chinese stew that will make your gizzard turn pale with joy. Refusing to be refused,

W. V. M.

To Daniel Gregory Mason

[NEW YORK, Jan. 31, 1899.]
[Postal card.]

Are you going to take those pants? It is important for me to know, as there are other customers. If a hasty decision (or the necessity of it) will prejudice the possibility of your coming, however, put it off until the ninth hour. You'd better come. Verbum sapienti. Pictures — music — theatre — dives — dinners — Broadway — Bowery — beer — girls — galoots — grippe — [the last word is stricken out] Heaven forefend! I've just come out of it.

W. V. M.

To Ferdinand Schevill

THE PLAYERS.
16 GRAMERCY PARK.
NEW YORK, Feb. 20, 1899.

DEAR FERD:

The great king Grippe reigns in Babylon, and his hand has been heavy on all his subjects — especially yours afflictedly. . . .

Are you still minded to woo the Muse under these skies in spring? There may be better places, but there surely are worse; and if the Muse though never so strictly meditated prove thankless, there yet remain Amaryllis and the tangles of Neaera's hair. The latter is usually a wig, but very nicely tangled and adequate for most purposes of distraction.

. . . . . .

WILL.

Address, 318 West 57th St.

To Daniel Gregory Mason

ATLANTIC TRANSPORT LINE, S. S. MESABA.
NEW YORK, March 11. [1899.]

DEAR DAN:

This is only a word to say that I have been unable to resist the very low rates of passage brought about by the rate-war between the transatlantic lines, and am off for England. . . . I shall settle down and work steadily. . . .

Hastily,

W. V. M.

To Ferdinand Schevill

36 GUILFORD ST., W. C.
LONDON, April 21. [1899.]

DEAR FERD:

I have been away from London, hunting for the wisdom of the thrush, so that your letter reaches me late. I hasten to assure you that you need n't be afraid of missing April's careless rapture; it's warranted not to be subject to draft this year before May. We have had next to no spring as yet, and if you girded up your pajamas and came across next month you would get both overture and tuning-up. Seriously, why can't you? Fares are so low that it's cheaper to come than stay, and we could have some rememberable hours: the country promises to be ravishing in a week or two more, and is already good. Walking from Wraysbury to Horton yesterday (a distance of 2½ miles across the fields) I counted eleven sky-larks, all soaring and singing fit to break your heart. . . .

To Daniel Gregory Mason

LONDON, May 13, 1899.

DEAR DAN:

. . . The Masque is done, all but the finishing touches and one song which wont get itself written straight. I have one or two small projects on hand to the pursuit of which I intend to devote this next month. . . .

W. V. M.

To Daniel Gregory Mason

31 GRADUATE HALL,
CHICAGO, July 5, '99.

DEAR DAN:

If I had written to you as often as I have thought of you, especially since I heard of poor

III

Savage's death,[1] you would have had no cause to complain. The news came to me on the boat, and came with a strange solemnity there in the middle of the ocean. I do not know of anybody who could go beyond time — that "thing how slight!" [2] — with better hopes of contentment there. It must have been almost at the very hour of his death that Joe Stickney [3] and I sat talking of him in the twilight of a Paris spring afternoon, and reading some of his lines with certain hopes of the larger though surely no sweeter or purer work he was to do some day. I do not know why the death of a spiritual man, at least one who dies in youth, is so much more moving than that of another. One would expect it to be the contrary way: perhaps it is to the true understanding. Well, he has left

[1] Philip Henry Savage (1868–1899), a contemporary of Moody's at Harvard, who wrote poetry of remarkable delicacy and distinction.

[2] "Brother, Time is a thing how slight!
Day lifts and falls, and it is night.
Rome stands an hour, and the green leaf
Buds into being bright and brief.
For us, God has at least in store
One shining moment, less or more.
Seize, then, what mellow sun we may,
To light us in the darker day."

"Poems" of Philip Henry Savage. Small, Maynard & Co., 1901.

[3] Joseph Trumbull Stickney (1874–1904), another Harvard poet, whose poems Moody and others edited after his early death.

behind a half-dozen lyrics that will last as long as the nation, or longer. Let us be content with that, as he doubtless was.

I have no time now, in the rush of the opening quarter, to tell you about myself, except to say that I heeded your admonition and "dropped a book" as I came through New York.[1] Macmillan is reading it. I have n't much confidence that the poor little volume will ever see the light under such august patronage, but somebody or other will be found with an eye to the thanks of posterity and a proud contempt for the contemporary dollar, I hope. I shall know its present fate in a few weeks and will let you know promptly.

As for the Milton, it has I believe been out several weeks or months, though I have not yet seen a copy. If you want to learn what the New York Nation thinks of it, look in the columns of that sheet for the latter part of April. It does not leave enough of me to bury. I am told that other critics (Literature, the Dial, etc.) have been more plenteous in mercy, but I have n't had strength to look, after the Nation man-handling.

. . . .

[1] This must have been the "Poems," eventually published in 1901 by Houghton, Mifflin & Co.

To Mrs. C. H. Toy

CHICAGO, Sept. 25, 1899.

MY DEAR MRS. TOY:

If I were not socially irreclaimable I should have told you long before this how when I got back to London that home of depression and tedium did its accustomed work upon me, and how in despair I fled to the country, from whose absolute greenness and comparative sunshine not even you and Miss Goodwin could tempt me. It strikes me upon re-reading that sentence that I never achieved such a climax in the course of my expressive life before, the emphasis falling the more thunderously because of the contrast in the unamiable life about me to those gay and friendly Paris days. Especially that morning we spent in rambling talk in the Luxembourg gardens often comes back to me with a quite peculiar charm, for which the *décor* is not wholly responsible, but rather "the human heart by which we live."

I am looking forward with eagerness to Boston and Cambridge this winter. The longer I live the more grateful I feel for the good and tried friends that I made there, and that have so generously borne and foreborne. Earnestly yours,

WILLIAM VAUGHN MOODY.

P.S. Do you know Landor's Imaginary Conversation in which a General Mavrocordato figures? An ancestor of your man?

To Josephine Preston Peabody

THE QUADRANGLE CLUB.
CHICAGO, September 30, '99.

Your generous praise makes me rather shame-faced: you ought to keep it for something that counts. At least other people ought: you would find a bright ringing word, and the proportion of things would be kept. As for me I am doing my best to keep the proportion of things, in the midst of no-standards and a dreary dingy fog-expanse of darkened counsel. Bah! here I am whining in my third sentence, and the purpose of this note was not to whine, but to thank you for heart new-taken. I take the friendly words, (for I need them cruelly) and forget the inadequate occasion of them. I am looking forward with almost fever-ish pleasure to the new year, when I shall be among friendships which time, and absence, and half-estrangement have only made to shine with a more inward light; and when, so accompanied, I can make shift to think and live a little. Do not wait till then to say Welcome.   W. V. M.

SOME LETTERS OF

To Daniel Gregory Mason

THE QUADRANGLE CLUB.
CHICAGO, Nov. 27, 1899.

DEAR DAN:

. . . I have been and still am driven with work, so that when I get a half-hour's leisure I am too done up to put one idea to another. But a good time is coming, and right soon, thank God! I shall be in Boston by the end of the Christmas holidays — and then ho! for talk and talk and talk, wherein all arrears shall be cancelled. I am on the verge of a good fortune that I hardly dare write about, for fear the envious gods will snatch it away. If they do not, I shall be yours not only for this spring but also for the summer and a good slice of next year. Will let you know at once when the die is cast.[1] . . .

To Daniel Gregory Mason

THE QUADRANGLE CLUB.
CHICAGO, Dec. 2nd, 1899.

DEAR DAN:

Your magnificence in paying down instantly

[1] He was enabled to take a considerable holiday from the university by his receipts from the "History of English Literature"

116

and royally for my mangy little note compels me to snatch another moment to make a part of it clearer. The hint which I threw out as to the possibility of getting a long "vacation" (you'll see in a minute that it isn't to be altogether vacant) means, to wit, that I am about to conclude negotiations with one of two rival firms who are equally convinced of my transcendant abilities, for a history of English literature for High Schools. In one case I am to do the whole of it and in the other half, and I incline to the latter because of the natural jealousy I feel of my time just now. The half of the job I can do, I think, in the spare or slack time of a year, and have my mornings pretty free for better things. It will bring me in five hundred plunks on delivery and if successful ought to constitute a source of permanent though small income. If these negotiations turn out all right, and I get the percentage of royalty for which I am stickling, I am going to apply for as long a leave of absence as the authorities will allow me, perhaps a year and a half, as I think I can pull through that period on what I have saved or can easily earn. The summer I am

on which he presently began work, in collaboration with Mr. Lovett.

bound to have though the Heavens fall, or rather because they are not going to fall but remain as a fittingly modest framework to the spectacle of my felicity.

Your conjecture about my work last spring (with the implied reproof and warning) is partly well-founded. Not wholly; for though London oppressed me brutally I worked the Masque out to twice its previous proportions, and most of the new matter seems to bear the test of cold subsequent criticism. It is now four times as long as when you saw it in fragment. There are, counting re-writing and further development here and there, about five hundred lines to be added, which will leave it about the length of a substantial five-act play — large enough to make a tidy volume by itself, if I can implore or coerce any publisher into printing it. With the Schlatter play [1] I have done little more. It wont do as it is, and I don't see yet how to go about resmelting it, though I still believe there is something in it worth saving. This will be one of the tasks of the winter. My heart leaps up when I behold, A calendar on the sly. I don't trust myself to envisage the same with prepense, for fear of danger to furniture and window

[1] "The Faith Healer."

glass. Have just heard from Robinson,[1] who conveys some lyric gibberish of yours about apples — if that's the word, I can't make out his immoral fist with certainty. . . .

To Daniel Gregory Mason

[Postmarked: CHICAGO, Dec. 18, 1899.]

Put it behind thee, my boy; 't is a device of Satan — a whisper of the Demon of Unrest and Seller of Dead Sea Apples. For which belief I shall soon furnish (*viva voce*) argument. The Muses, I groundedly believe, reside at present on an obscure peak (not yet visited) of New Hampshire or Maine; that is, if they have not already succumbed to the attractions of Pike's Peak or Mount Shasta. At any rate that's where I purpose to seek them, and Europe be damned. I have spoken.   W. V. M.

Moody arrived in Boston at Christmas, and took a room in the Hermitage, No. 1 Willow St. It was here that, as I find recorded in my journal at the time, he finally completed "The Masque of Judgment," January 25, 1900. The "Ode in Time of Hesitation" was also written during this period, and appeared in the

---

[1] Edwin Arlington Robinson, author of "Captain Craig," "The Town Down the River," etc.

Atlantic Monthly for May. In the early spring he established himself at East Gloucester, Massachusetts, where he wrote "Gloucester Moors" and the "Menagerie," and revised the play dealing with Schlatter, the "New Mexico Messiah," which he read to a group of his friends at Falmouth, Mass., in July. During part of the summer he lived with his friend Mr. Truman H. Bartlett, in Chocorua, N. H. In October he was again settled in Willow St., but in November he went to New York, where he lived at 71 Irving Place until his return to Chicago in January, 1901, save for part of the Christmas holidays, spent with one of his sisters in Newton, Massachusetts.

During all this period, a most important one in his poetic development, he had to give a considerable portion of his time to the text-book on English literature, but managed to keep his mornings largely free for creative work. The period is notable for publication as well as for production: "The Masque of Judgment" was printed by Small, Maynard & Co. in November, 1900, and the "Poems" appeared in May, 1901, under the imprint of Houghton, Mifflin & Co.

To Robert Morss Lovett

1 WILLOW ST.
BOSTON, March 22, 1900.

DEAR ROB:

I have just finished the early (Pre-Chaucerian) portion of the greatest critical commentary of modern times, and in view of my struggles therewith your jaunty proposition to have your half of the job done by midsummer, and teaching to boot, fills me with envy. To be sure I had forgotten all my Anglo-Saxon and never knew any Middle English, and had to grub like hell to get at the stuff in some respectably first-hand way; but that this chapter should have taken me six solid weeks of my precious vacation breaks my heart.

. . . .

As ever,

WILL.

To Daniel Gregory Mason

THE HARBOR VIEW, EAST GLOUCESTER,
April 6, [1900.]

DEAR DAN:

I have put off writing you in order to give this place a thorough test and report definitely upon it as a vacation resort. I have liked it from the first and like it better the longer I stay. The humors of the harbor are many and its picturesqueness inexhaustible. The moors, which stretch for several miles to the eastward, are beautiful in color and form, and the coast, although not rugged, is very diversified. The house itself is as good a country inn as I ever saw. . . . There are a good many girls here now and are likely to be until after the Easter vacation; but they will let you alone if you insist. . . .

Let me know at once if you will venture it for the holidays, as I may have to bespeak your room in advance. I have hunted out some glorious walks and believe that — if you can bring books enough to beguile your mornings and evenings — we can have a first-rate time.

W. V. M.

P.S. There is a ghastly piano: fortunately it is *so* ghastly that few of our *virtuosi* brave its terrors.

To Daniel Gregory Mason

THE HARBOR VIEW
[EAST GLOUCESTER, April 11, 1900.]

DEAR DAN:

The room is all right, whether you come Saturday or Monday. Perhaps if you want to like the place you had better wait till Monday to avoid getting your first impression under the Sunday blight; but you best know your own fortitude. Bring outing duds, of course: possibly a boiled shirt for evenings, if you're haughty. . . . If you come in the afternoon, and will let me know when, I will meet you at the station. If I am not there take trolley car which passes station, labelled Rocky (not Rubber) Neck, and tell the conductor to put you off at the Harbor View. It is a two-mile ride, over a very tempestuous road-bed. Bring *heavy shoes*, if possible waterproof, as the moors are apt to be dampish in the low places and we don't want to have to keep to the roads. A cap is an absolute necessity for comfort in shore tramps.

W. V. M.

To Robert Morss Lovett

HARBOR VIEW INN.
GLOUCESTER, MASS., April 30.

DEAR ROB:

Tomorrow would seem to be the first of May, and I am sending, according to agreement, the three chapters of the text-book which I have blocked out. They are in first draft and I fear not very legible in all places, but there is no type-writer in this village and I had n't the heart to copy those hundred and ten weary pages. You can easily decipher enough to afford grounds for a curse-out.

123

I should especially like to have criticism as to proportion; I find this the most difficult matter to gauge and adjust. In general, I realize that the Anglo-Saxon chapter and the chapter on the drama before Shakespeare are both too long. I think I can cut them down some in rewriting.

I am convinced by the part I have done that we must make a great effort to keep the thing simple and broad. To do this without falling into the stick-candy style is hard; I realize that in many places I have been narrow and mixed, in my struggles to convey some little nutriment of fact in the kissing-comfits of generalization.

. . . .

As you will see by the postmark I have fled Beacon Hill and set up my everlasting rest by the sea. This little fishing village is a bewitching place, and the country about, to the extremest tip of Cape Ann, is as good as Brittany. . . .

As ever yours,

W. V. M.

WILLIAM VAUGHN MOODY

To Mary L. Mason

HARBOR VIEW INN.
GLOUCESTER, MASS.,
May 1st, 1900.

MY DEAR MRS. MASON:

. . . .

Gloucester continues to be almost too good to
be true. Dan and I had a capital ten days together, but the orchestra was only tuning up then;
now the first theme is being given out, high, high
in the violins. *Pace* Apthorp.[1]

Mr. C—— is a good man and true: he scorns
the doctrine that discretion is the better part of
friendship. Of such are the kingdom of heaven.

Earnestly yours,
W. V. MOODY.

To Mary L. Mason

THE HARBOR VIEW.
EAST GLOUCESTER, MASS.
May 16, 1900.

DEAR MRS. MASON:

Your invitation is very tempting, though as far
as the Gloucester spring is concerned I'm willing

---

[1] W. F. Apthorp, who was at that time compiling the analyt-
ical program books of the Boston Symphony Orchestra.

to back it for handsomeness even against the Milton variety. Promptly at 9 o'clock each morning I put on blinders, stuff my ears with wax, and strap myself to the desk, in order to do my day's stint on a text-book on English Literature (God save the mark!) which I have to get a certain portion of done this month. . . .

Faithfully yours,
WILLIAM VAUGHN MOODY.

To Daniel Gregory Mason

[Undated. Probably May or June, 1900.]

DEAR DAN:

I will answer as categorically as you inquire:

1st. I beseech you to come.

2nd. I will join you at luncheon on the beach,[1] and offer my services as guide, philosopher, and friend.

3rd. I will not read the Ode, the Faith-Healer, nor any other damned thing under the shining canopy. I will talk with you, walk with you, play with you, and stay with you, and so following; but I will not read for you nor bleed for you. What news on the Rialto?

W. V. M.

[1] A small picnic party was proposed.

WILLIAM VAUGHN MOODY

To Daniel Gregory Mason

PROUT'S NECK. [MAINE.]
June 23, 1900.

DEAR DAN:

. . . The only hotel open in the place is this one, the Checkley, which I tackled in despair after knocking in vain at the doors of several less imposing hostelries. I was agreeably surprised to find I could get a small but fairly comfortable room here for ten plunks per. . . . The high piazzas command a great view of the bay and open sea. . . . Of the eighteen people now here, I am the only one who could be called a star, but there are prospects of a more or less stellar sort for the immediate future. The place is so roomy that I don't believe the non-stellar people will get on our nerves. . . . If you decide to come, as I hope, the following is the manner.

Boat leaves India Wharf at 7 P.M. Be on hand by 6.15 in order to get stateroom. Fare (including stateroom) to Portland, $2.00. Go to bed early, for she gets into Portland Harbor long before dawn and there is thenceforward a hell of a noise unloading things. You can stay in bed until 7, and breakfast on the boat. Take street car passing wharf, marked Union Station, which will deposit you in front of the ticket window. Ask politely the man behind the window to give you a ticket to Scarboro Beach, price sixteen cents. At Scarboro Beach (*not* Scarboro Crossing) you will find a stage running to this hotel, a four mile ride for which you pay 50 cents. With these few hints to guide you, and the exercise of your native sagacity and presence of mind in peril, you will arrive.

Be of good courage, and come. Don't forget your bathing suit.

Yours,

W. V. M.

To Daniel Gregory Mason

CHOCORUA, N. H.

July 29th, 1900.

DEAR DAN:

Immediately on my arrival I was swooped down upon by Mr. Bartlett, and soon transferred bag and baggage to his house, where I am living in undisturbed possession of the upper story. We get our own breakfast and take dinner and supper at the hotel. He wants me to say that when you come next week he hopes you will join us. I think we could have a very jolly time together. The old boy is in marvellous form, and stars the passing hours with immortal phrases.

As ever,

WILL.

To Robert Morss Lovett

CHOCORUA, N. H.
Aug. 18th, 1900.

DEAR ROB:

I am, as you see, at Chocorua, and expect to be here about two weeks longer. . . . I am working now on the Milton period; have it something more than half done.

I am staying with a Mr. Bartlett, ex-sculptor, art critic, and in spite of all a magnificent old goat and man of God.

.   .   .   .

Yours,

W. V. M.

To Edmund Clarence Stedman

1 WILLOW STREET,
BOSTON, Oct. 30, 1900.

MY DEAR MR. STEDMAN:

I give myself the pleasure of sending, in advance

129

of publication, The Masque of Judgment, about which I wrote you a word or two last spring. Doubtless you are overwhelmed with tributes of this questionable kind, yet I am bold enough to hope you will read the book, even if it remains in your mind as a symbol of grotesquely ambitious "first volumes."

Another copy, properly bound, will be sent on publication, the second week of November.

Believe me
Very earnestly yours,
WILLIAM VAUGHN MOODY.

To Daniel Gregory Mason

SALMAGUNDI CLUB.
14 WEST 12th ST., N. Y.
Nov. 14, 1900.

DEAR DAN:

. . . I am pretty lonely here, as Robinson has gone to Hoboken or Spuytenduyvil or somewhere, to live with the goats, and I only see him once a week. For a few days I thought the noise would drive me wild, and I was more than once on the point of fleeing back to the Hermitage, which by comparison seems to the fond eye of memory to deserve its name. There are three hundred and twenty-three hand-organs and ninety-seven pianos on our block, and every hour thirty-five thousand drays loaded with sheet iron pass the house. Irving Place, you know, is a quiet old-fashioned neighborhood, so we are justly proud of these slight evidences of animation.

The theatres (which are after all what I came for) are good, and a great resource. . . .

WILL.

My address is 71 Irving Place.

To Mary L. Mason

THE PLAYERS.
16 GRAMERCY PARK.
NEW YORK, Nov. 30, 1900.

MY DEAR MRS. MASON:

I am sorry that you found the upshot of the Masque (I mean its main drift and meaning) negative or destructive. I did not intend it to be so. For me the kernel of the thing was Raphael's humanistic attitude and Uriel's philosophy, especially his "confession of faith" in Act III, Scene II. The rest of it was only mythological machinery for exhibiting the opposed attitude and philosophy — that of the deniers of life. I hoped that the positive meaning might disengage itself as a kind of aroma or emotion from the whole, and that the poem would thus subserve just such a brave love of life and faith in its issues as you plead for. If this does not happen for the sympathetic reader, then I have failed wholly.

Your praise of the manner of the poem I am grateful for, especially as it came at a moment of deep discouragement. Believe me,

Always faithfully yours,

WILLIAM VAUGHN MOODY.

To Daniel Gregory Mason

THE PLAYERS.
16 GRAMERCY PARK.
NEW YORK, NOV. 30, 1900.

DEAR DAN:

Your generous praise of the Masque gave me great joy, for I was going through a crisis of discouragement which made my months of labor and engrossment upon it seem pitiably futile. I am alarmed about myself, when I notice that the fluctuations of heaven-scaling confidence and something very like despair, instead of decreasing as they ought to do, seem to increase with my years and knowledge. I don't understand it at all, nor do I see any way of combating it that promises much.

Your sister [in-law] has just written, and from her tone I gather that she found the total impression of the book rather gloomy and pessimistic. I'm afraid I have n't made clear enough the positive part — the love of life and belief in its issues — which I meant to be the core of the matter. How do you feel about it?

. . . .

Always yours,

WILL.

To Mrs. C. H. Toy

CENTURY CLUB, NEW YORK.
DECEMBER 12, 1900.

DEAR MRS. TOY:

Your objection to the "theology" of the Masque would be well taken if there were any theology in it. There is n't an ounce, or at least if there is it is there against my will. Of course I did n't intend my "strangely unpleasant" God to be taken seriously. To me the whole meaning and value of the poem lies in the humanistic attitude and character of Raphael, the philosophic outlook of Uriel, and the plea for passion as a means of salvation everywhere latent. The rest

133

of it is only mythological machinery for symboliz-
ing the opposed doctrine — that of the denial of
life. As Christianity (contrary of course to the
wish and meaning of its founder) has historically
linked itself with this doctrine, I included certain
aspects of it in this mythological apparatus —
always with a semi-satirical intention. I meant to
write a poem, pure and simple; and my western
friends, with the naiveté proper to them, seem to
have accepted it as such; but Cambridge insists
on treating it as a theological treatise. As such,
they can but find it pretty foolish, I fear. . . .

From the time of Moody's return to Chicago at the
beginning of 1901 his letters, much less frequent and
voluminous than formerly, leave many gaps in the
record of his life. He was now able to get longer leaves
of absence from his teaching, and spent much time in
travelling, both in America and in Europe. His love
of wild life led him to the Rocky Mountains with
Mr. Hamlin Garland in the summer of 1901, and to
Arizona, alone, in the spring of 1904 — excursions
which later bore fruit in his first published prose play,
"The Great Divide." He made a trip to Greece in
1902. The rest of this period he divided between
Boston, New York, and Chicago. The chief literary
event was the publication of his second poetic drama,
"The Fire-Bringer," in March, 1904.

WILLIAM VAUGHN MOODY

To Daniel Gregory Mason

CHICAGO, Jan. 16, 1901.

DEAR DAN:

Many thanks for the post-card containing extract from Robinson's letter. Such words from him cannot but give me immense satisfaction, both because he is a man who weighs his words and because they apply in this case to a kind of writing with which he has n't much patience in general (I mean the "history of the world" kind of thing) so that I don't feel compelled in honesty to discount for personal bias. Well, he can afford to be generous.

It has been the very devil to get down to work again, after my long and keenly relished holiday. Chicago seemed uglier and grimmer than I had believed possible. There was nothing to do but shut my eyes, put my sensibilities in the lower bureau drawer, and sail in. Gradually the beneficent numbness of drudgery is stealing over me, and that unilluminated dogged patience which constitutes my substitute for moral courage is beginning to possess what in other seasons I am wont to refer to exuberantly as my soul. It is at such times as this that I envy you most keenly your unflinching hold upon spiritual truth, and your power of walking in the light of it. The best I can do is to hump my back, turn down my hat brim, and stoically count the number of streams running down my back, until the damned drizzle decides to cease. . . .

Write when you feel like it, and don't till you do. I mean do when you do rather than don't. That is to say do do and don't don't. See?

WILL.

To Edwin Arlington Robinson

THE QUADRANGLE CLUB.
CHICAGO, Jan. 24, 1901.

DEAR ROBINSON:

You will not have thought it was indifference to your "poor words of congratulation" about the Masque which has kept me from answering sooner. What you said gave me the deepest — joy, I was going to say; but remembering your distrust of exuberant language, I will say satisfaction. Still, it was joy, all the same — the feeling was exuberant enough to warrant, this once, my florid vocabulary. Your words were the more grateful because they came as a surprise. I thought in New York that you were bravely trying to be generous (you would have said "just") toward a thing you rootedly deplored but suspected yourself of being by nature prejudiced against. As you had more than done your duty on this hypothesis, I could not but consider this later testimony as being the voice of the natural man, speaking the faith that was in him; and therefore I rejoiced.

Chicago is several kinds of hell, but I won't weary you with asseverations that I am being shamefully victimized by fate; you won't believe it, and besides it's a lie. I am merely paying the market rates for my bread and beer, commodities for which many a better man has been villainously overcharged. Some of the vacation memories I most like to hark back to and mouse dreamily over are those walks we had from Riverdale to Yonkers, especially the last one. This is n't a letter, but it would be a pleasant fiction and a graceful act for you to consider it so, and write me one.

Always yours,

W. V. M.

SOME LETTERS OF

To Mrs. C. H. Toy

CHICAGO,
March 2, 1901.

DEAR MRS. TOY:

. . . Life here is as ever. More different kinds
of a mistake and an affliction than you can dream
— you there in that gentle elegiac Cambridge.
Not that I would give up my journey through the
realms of woe; I am learning a lot down here, and
each descending circle of the lamentable pit makes
me surer that I did well to come. But ah, I long
for a Virgil to comment and illuminate the thing
now and then! Even Dante had to be personally
conducted through hell, and I guess he was right
smart more of a hero than what I be. It's melting
outside today, and the sun is doing a South
Halstead street bunco game on a confiding world.
Here is a poem inspired by my last attempt to
wade the street:

> Gutters sing.
> Is it spring?
> Does old Winter
> Now beginter
> Quit?
> Nit!

138

WILLIAM VAUGHN MOODY

> Long time yet,
> You bet,
> Ere G. S.[1]
> Comes to bless
> Us. I guess
> Yes.

These "Thoughts on a Thaw" I think of submitting as my contribution to the next edition of *The Poets of Indiana: an Anthology;* just published by Macmillan. At present I'm not represented, but I'll force them to recognize me yet.

To Daniel Gregory Mason

WAGON WHEEL GAP.
COLORADO, Aug. 30, 1901.

DEAR DAN:

If to do were as easy as to know what 't were good to do, I should not have thus neglected the best of friends and good fellows. Your two letters and the picture reached me — I am ashamed to think how many months ago, and I was too low in my mind even to send a word of goodbye on your departure for Paris. I waved a loving, if dispirited, farewell from the central core of Chicago's smoke

---

[1] Gentle Spring.

cloud, and in that infernal seat of contemplation have often mused upon your goings and comings in the Latin Quarter. *J'ai pauvre. Nous partons aujourd'hui.* By pronouncing these mysterious formulae I have many times evoked you in confrontation with that so elusive world of will and idea which we once endeavored to comprehend together and found and shall find entirely incomprehensible. . . .

At present, as the superscription of this scrawl will show you, I am in the wilds of the Rockies, where I have been camping and trailing with Hamlin Garland, in some of the savagest old country these States afford. Garland had the bad luck to get his foot crushed (his horse fell on it in scrambling out of a bog up a steep bank) and he is laid up for a week or two. Meantime I am doing some of the mountain passes on horseback, riding from thirty to fifty miles a day, trying to get the stale taste of a year's *academica* out of my mouth.

I am free now for a year. I shall stay west (somewhere near Chicago) until I get that wretched text-book done (this time it has got to be done!). . . . This scrawl is all I am up to just now, after a hard day's ride and last night spent sleeplessly in a deserted mountain hut with three or four other benighted travellers. Travellers is euphemistic: with the doubtful exception of myself they were tramps — miners out of a job hoboing it to a new mining camp. And downright good fellows they were, too, barring the absence of certain niceties of person — which, indeed, our somewhat casual quarters were not calculated to encourage. If by good luck this finds you at Chocorua, greet for me the Grand Old Man and his pals the mountains. Cull for me a morning phrase, big as Whiteface and dewy as those morning glories on the projected and now I trust realized pergola. I grow disproportioned. But cull it for me natheless (as the Bard would say) and send it to me along with an account of yourself in all the moods and tenses.

Always yours,

W. V. M.

To Mary L. Mason

1 WILLOW ST.
[Boston.] Dec. 27 [1901].

MY DEAR MRS. MASON:

It was immensely kind of you to remember me on Christmas day. I have been munching the ginger as I work, and eagerly watching for some effect on my style. Did you send it in that hope? If so, I trust that means you are sufficiently interested in the fate of the text-book to be willing to do some more typewriting for it. . . . Will you let me know whether to send you more MS., and also will you send me a memorandum of what we owe you for the two chapters on the novel?

. . . .

Yours,

W. V. M.

To Josephine Preston Peabody

1 Willow St.
Jan. 5, 1902.

Dear J. P. P.,

I am not going to apologize for not telling you so sooner, but am going to tell you at once and to your face that I think the Play ["Marlowe"] is a beauty. For honest beauty and wisdom and strength it beats Stephen Phillips and the rest of them out of the world. Your blank verse has strengthened incalculably since Fortune and M. E. It has just the clearness, grip, and nervousness I have been looking for it to attain. The ventriloquism of your dialogue impresses me more at each reading — a great and hard thing to achieve in

blank verse. I can count on one hand the drama-
tists who have learned that trick of mirroring
character — mental status — etc., in the move-
ment of a blank verse line. Your Marlowe is a
woman's Marlowe, but all the better for that.
He is what he ought to have been and perhaps
essentially was, underneath, though I doubt if he
found it out — probably went to the dogs for not
finding it out. Your Alison is a man's Alison, and
all the better for that! (Only a man would never
call her "the Little Quietude," and I wish you
had n't. I know I'm a brute for not liking that
and the "shrine" business, but I don't.) But all
the figures are greatly energized — snap fire when
you touch them — and Marlowe is full of those
brave translunary things that the first poets had.
By all the Muses, we shall have an American
drama yet, and it will date from Marlowe: a
Play.

I have been living in a night-mare since I got
here, and have seen no one. The strain is nearly
over, and I am beginning to remember once more
that this world is after all a real world, full of such
good things as friends and friendly talk. I am
coming out to see you in a day or two, and you
must n't shut the door on me because my manners

are bad. My heart is a good heart, and wears Kentish russet —

W. V. M.

To Mary L. Mason

1 WILLOW ST.

BOSTON, Jan. 27, 1902.

MY DEAR MRS. MASON:

Your word of praise for the poor text-book was most cheering; I shall hope and trust, after this, that it is n't as bad as it seems to me. It lies on my spirit like Incubus.

. . . Your feminine mathematics juggled you out of about fifteen hundred words on your last count. Thank God that you are dealing with a just man, and forswear addition: it is a vain thing for safety.

Always yours,

W. V. M.

To Daniel Gregory Mason

MACKINAC ISLAND, MICH.

Oct. 22, 1903.

DEAR DAN:

Rumor vaguely reports you as domiciled at the Benedick, and my hopes that you are so are too strong to allow me to doubt. I have spent the summer on this little island in Lake Huron, finishing the poem of which I read you the beginning (you may remember) last winter.[1] I have often thought of you and wondered where you were. Now that winter and return to city life is at hand, and the possibility of my spending said winter in New York is good, my eagerness to hear from you, and if the good fates will permit me, to get quarters within hearing distance of your voice and your piano, reaches the point of epistolary explosion — as you know, a high point with me, . . .

To Josephine Preston Peabody

CHICAGO, March 22 [1904].

DEAR J. P. P.:

I was sorry not to see you again, especially if you were primed with talk about It; for I, as always, am wearying to know about It, but seem daily farther from achieving knowledge. The more I have to do with It, the more It escapes my thought and definition. I don't mean to imply that you were going to think or define, but I suspect that you were going to throw out memorable speech, while revolving invisible with illumination upon your stellar axis.

[1] Probably "The Fire-Bringer."

I am hesitating whether or not to go to the Great Desert of Arizona and live with the Indians and "lung-ers" this spring. Probably I shall go. If I never come back, but stay and choose some savage woman to rear my dusky race, remember that I intended a copy of the Fire-Eater [sic] for you, with a handsome inscription.   Yours,

W. V. M.

To Edwin Arlington Robinson

HOTEL BALTIMORE.
KANSAS CITY, MO., March 29, 1904.

DEAR ROBINSON:

Behold me *en route* for Arizona, the Painted Desert, and aboriginal life. . . .

The Fire-Eater [The Fire-Bringer] reached me just a minute before I left Chicago, and I had time only to scratch your initials on the fly-leaf of a copy, and forgot to leave your address behind; nevertheless, the little book (of which I suspect you heartily disapprove, for reasons) will reach you in due course.

.   .   .   .

Always yours,

W. V. M.

146

WILLIAM VAUGHN MOODY

To Daniel Gregory Mason

KANSAS CITY, Mo.
March 29, 1904.

DEAR DAN:

I am a thousand times obliged for your friendly offices in negotiating the lease and sending on my stuff. After I wrote I became conscience-stricken over the magnitude of the trouble I had put you to; but the chance I had for going to Arizona and seeing some aboriginal life was exceptional, and I could not afford to go on to New York to make the arrangements myself; at least to do so would have so seriously depleted my funds that I should probably have had to abandon the western trip after said arrangements had been made. I do not see what you get out of it except the good man's ancient reward (too much relied upon by putters of others to trouble) and the satisfaction of having —— near at hand and in pleasant quarters. I have written urging him to occupy the room, and told him to apply to you for the key to the bureau. . . . My book[1] turned up (advanced copies) just as I was leaving the house to take the western train; I had time to put your initials on a fly-leaf, and

[1] "The Fire-Bringer."

147

M. L. M's on another, and they ought to reach you in a day or two. I shall drop you a line now and then from the shadow of a giant-cactus or from the top of a Zuni pueblo.

Ever yours,

W. V. M.

P.S. No, Chicago has not been chucked, merely happily relegated to the future.

To Percy MacKaye

2970 GROVELAND AVE.,

CHICAGO, Aug. 5, 1904.

MY DEAR MR. MACKAYE,

Let me thank you very heartily for your generous words concerning "The Fire-Bringer." Such words would be very pleasant to hear from any one, and they are trebly so when that one is a fellow-workman in the poetic drama. It is true, as Mr. Shipman has told you, that I am heart and soul dedicated to the conviction that modern life can be presented on the stage in the poetic mediums, and adequately presented only in that way. If I am anywhere near Cornish this summer, as is not improbable, it will give me genuine pleasure to look you up. In any case you will find me from the first of November on, at 51 West 10th

WILLIAM VAUGHN MOODY

Street, New York; and I hope that you will come
to see me there. With thanks and good wishes,
I am   Earnestly yours
                    WM. VAUGHN MOODY.
PERCY MACKAYE ESQ.

To Daniel Gregory Mason

51 WEST 10th St.
NEW YORK, Oct. 8, 1904.
DEAR DAN:

. . . .

I got your quotation about St. Lô and the Val
de Vire, and was delighted with it, as I should
have assured you if you had given me an address.
By the way, I have put "Old Pourquoi" (do you
remember?) into a poem, which I think will
amuse you.

. . . .

W. V. M.

To Edmund Clarence Stedman

2970 GROVELAND AVE.
CHICAGO, Jan. 12, 1905.
MY DEAR MR. STEDMAN:
Your letter has followed me deviously through
the south and north again, with its most friendly

message. That you should have taken the trouble to write me at such length and with your own hand gives double worth to the news of my nomination for membership in the Institute. As for this latter let me say at once that I am grateful to you for proposing my name, and if elected shall accept the honor gladly. Your generous words concerning my "Fire-Bringer" have given me great joy. The poem got little praise, and that little mostly misdirected, so that I had come to think of it, as — so far as my hoped-for audience was concerned — a failure. But if you like it, it is no failure, and I can go on with a good heart. It is a vast pity you did not carry out your intention of treating the theme yourself. It takes some generosity to feel so, since your poem would have rendered mine superfluous, if not impertinence. But I am at bottom more jealous for Poetry, and especially for the poetry which shall be named and recognized as in a large sense American, than I am for my own poems, though jealous enough for them, Heaven knows, according to the flesh! Your beautiful Alectryôn, taken in connection with what you tell me of your thwarted intention, shows how parlously near I came to having my theme "assumed" into a heaven of invention where I should neither have dared nor wished to pursue it. You have my — so to speak — "post humorous" gratitude, with the reservation named. I am particularly glad that you do not share the current prejudice against such subjects, in favor of a literary Americanism which I, for my own part, cannot but deem false in theory and barren in practice. . . . Believe me, Faithfully yours,

WILLIAM VAUGHN MOODY.

The studio at 51 West 10th St., occupied by a friend during the Arizona trip, made a convenient New York headquarters, which Moody retained for some time. He was back there in the fall of 1904, and through the following spring. His work was now eagerly sought by some of the magazines, and one of the pleasantest friendships of this time was that with Richard Watson Gilder of the *Century*. Mr. Gilder's poem, referred to in the letters, was printed in the *Atlantic Monthly* for June, 1905, under the title, "A New Poet."

A NEW POET

BY R. W. GILDER

I

FRIENDS, beware!
Stop babbling! Hark, a sound is in the air!
Above the pretty songs of schools
(Not of music made, but rules),

Above the panic rush for gold
And emptinesses manifold,
And selling of the soul for phantom fame,
And reek of praises where there should be blame;
Over the dust and muck,
The buzz and roar of wheels,
Another music steals, —
A right, true note is struck.

II

Friends, beware!
A sound of singing in the air!
The love song of a man who loves his fellow men;
Mother-love and country-love, and the love of sea
    and fen;
Lovely thoughts and mighty thoughts and thoughts
    that linger long;
There has come to the old world's singing the thrill
    of a brave new song.

III

They said there were no more singers,
But listen! — A master voice!
A voice of the true joy-bringers!
Now will ye heed and rejoice,
Or pass on the other side,
And wait till the singer hath died,
Then weep o'er his voiceless clay?
Friends, beware!

WILLIAM VAUGHN MOODY

A keen, new sound is in the air, —
Know ye a poet's coming is the old world's judgment day!

To Richard Watson Gilder

51 WEST 10TH ST.
NEW YORK, April 17 [1905].

DEAR MR. GILDER,

. . . .

At the risk of seeming ungracious, and insensi-
ble of the honor which you have planned to do
me, I am going to ask you to publish the poem in
the Atlantic without my initials. I do so because
of no boyish mock-modesty, but because I know
in the bottom of my heart that I have not yet
reached a point in the practice of our divine art
which entitles me to this sort of public recognition from a man like you. Even if you are ardently
and generously minded enough to think otherwise, I beg that you will yield to my own deep
feeling in the matter, which I express only after
long thought. Try to ascribe my rejection of the
offered honor to a sentiment no less magnanimous
than was the one which prompted you to extend
it, and believe me

Always faithfully yours,
WM. VAUGHN MOODY.

153

To Richard Watson Gilder

51 WEST 10TH ST.
NEW YORK, April 19th.

DEAR MR. GILDER,

I am grateful to you for acceding to my request about the initials, and for understanding my motive. I am also much obliged to you for the sight of your letter to Traubel about the Whitman letters. Whitman did himself sore wrong in many of his judgments — but for the matter of that so do we all. It is good to rise above personal injustice as you do in your lines written for the dinner, which I return (together with the letter) with thanks for the privilege of seeing them.

· · · · · · · · ·

To Richard Watson Gilder

51 WEST 10TH ST.
NEW YORK, Thursday.

DEAR MR. GILDER,

The poem made me very proud and happy, and I shall preserve it among my most cherished possessions, both for its generous personal praise and for its intrinsic beauty. I have made the correction of which you speak.

· · · · · · · · ·

154

WILLIAM VAUGHN MOODY

To Richard Watson Gilder

[Posted April 27, 1905.]

DEAR MR. GILDER:

I scribble this lying on my back in the hospital, where on Friday last I underwent an operation which proved rather serious. I did not tell you about it and do not send you the address now because I know that your native kindness would lead you to take all sorts of trouble about it, and my own instinct is just to lie low and not peep until nature restores me again to an upright posture and the self-respect thereunto appertaining. I am well looked after, and getting along capitally under the circumstances. I started this note to thank you for letting me see Robinson's note, and to say that I would send you a poem or two for inspection when I get up again.

I know you must be terribly cut up over Jefferson's death. Yours,

W. V. M.

To Edwin Arlington Robinson

33 EAST 33RD ST.,
NEW YORK, May 10 [1905].

DEAR ROBINSON,

Your note of inquiry and expostulation reached

me some days ago, but I have hardly been up to writing before today. I am happy to report that the operation which I underwent three weeks ago has succeeded admirably, and I shall soon be on my feet again — at least on one of them and a cane or two. For the first few days after they sliced me I had a squeak for it; temperature anything in the shade and pulse hopping like a jackrabbit who descries Teddy on the horizon. However, Nature soon decided that I was of more use to her in an organized state than as phosphates, and since then I have made a rapid recovery. . . .

To Richard Watson Gilder

51 WEST 10TH ST.
May 13th, 1905.

DEAR MR. GILDER,

Yes, I am out of the hospital, thank God, owing to my flat refusal to endure any longer the hideous monotony of blank walls and blank hours (the latter my own fault, I know), but I am not yet very much master of my machine — only able to hobble tentatively about on one leg and a cane or two.

· · · · · · · · ·

I do not want to go away for the summer without seeing you again, for who knows where either of us will be by the time the leaves fall? If you wish, I will bring a few verses to read, but I do not think that I have anything suitable for the magazine. If I am to do this I must read them to you *solus* (this you will grant to my constitutional fear of an "audience").

Thanks for St. Gaudens' note. It is pleasant to possess anything from the hand of that noble artist.

Faithfully yours,
WM. VAUGHN MOODY.

Mrs. Gilder puts me under another debt by a second jar of that delectable coagulation.

W. V. M.

To Mary L. Mason

51 WEST 10TH ST.
Monday. [Postmark, June 5, 1905.]

DEAR MARY MASON,

Though I must sorrowfully confess to having been "beguiled" by no dames, yet so beguiling a note as yours of this morning is a sufficient recompense. My sister has watched over me with so hawklike an eye, to prevent me from overexerting my lame leg, that I have not been able to escape as far as your house. This week I shall make another and more desperate attempt to run the blockade, and in case of success shall drop in upon you some evening to swap operation-stories. . . . You must not look to find me the picture of grace — the pardlike spirit beautiful and swift — that I once was. . . .

W. V. M.

To Richard Watson Gilder

2970 GROVELAND AVE.,
CHICAGO, ILL., Aug. 23, '05.

DEAR MR. GILDER,

The account of "housework" in your country, and especially your contribution to the cere-monies, gave me the keenest pleasure. I am an ancient and — as I thought — irreconcilable enemy of the Whitmanic verse-mode, but your handling of it goes far to prove me wrong and baptize me into the new dispensation. The bee-filled linden-tree, "humming . . . like the plucked string of a violin," is unforgettably good. As regards the "Second Coming" I would say to the possible illustrator that the caulking-man was a strong, sensual-looking young Greek of the island type, naked to the waist, with cropped hair and bare feet; the person speaking to him was curiously spiritual in feature, slightly bearded, bare-headed, dressed in the long flowing gown of the Greek priesthood, rusty black in tone. He looked like an Armenian. I will try to clarify the "watery death" stanza, either by distillation or plain sopping up.

The President's *Outlook* article was undeniably kind in intention and will doubtless do Robinson much worldly good. As for its substance, since we have adopted the absolute despotic form of government I deem it best that such treasonable matter as criticism of the imperial utterances, even on such a trifling subject as poetry, be not committed to ink. I have no taste for labor in the mines of Siberia — I mean Alaska — with a ball and chain on my left leg.

Various circumstances make it difficult for me to go East as I had intended, but I may go on later. If so I shall surely give myself the pleasure of seeing you at Four Brooks. Sincerely yours,

WM. VAUGHN MOODY.

"The President's *Outlook* article" was a very complimentary review by Colonel Roosevelt of Mr. Edwin Arlington Robinson's "Captain Craig."

Early in 1906 Moody finished his prose play, "The Great Divide," which received some trial performances that spring in Chicago under the title "A Sabine Woman," and was regularly put on the stage the following fall, in New York, by Miss Margaret Anglin and Mr. Henry Miller. The opening night was October 4th.

To Richard Watson Gilder

51 West 10th St.
New York, Feb. 5 [1906].

Dear Mr. Gilder,

I do not know what the scope or function of the MacDowell Club is, so that I cannot tell whether my new play ["The Great Divide"] would be suitable for its stage or not. I am anxious to get it produced on the professional stage, by a professional troupe. Miss Marlowe and Sothern, however, I am sure would not cotton to it, as it is "realism" of a rather grim and uncompromising type, without the romantic glamor which they affect — at least what romantic glamor there is is implicit and present only to the probing eye of the elect. I should very much like to get Henry Miller to take it, but I guess that is out of the question. The "Fire-Bringer" — if all plans go through — is to be produced next winter in

Chicago, in a new theatre which is being started there.

. . . .

To Percy MacKaye

HOTEL SEVILLE, NEW YORK CITY,
Oct. 11, 1906.

DEAR PERCY,

Thanks for your cordial note about the play. Broadway the formidable has indeed roared us as any sucking dove, for this once. It's like taking candy from a child. I am making my plans to get down to Philadelphia for your opening. Save me à ticket, and I shall come if it's a possible thing.

Faithfully yours,

WILL.

To Daniel Gregory Mason

[NEW YORK.]
Oct. 12, 1906.

DEAR DAN,

I had tickets in my pocket for you and Mary, for the opening night of the play, and hoped you would turn up to use them. When you did n't I consoled myself with the reflection that, in case the thing was a failure, you would be spared pain, and I also, by your absence. When, at the end of the first act, it looked like a go, and still more when, after the second, the audience rose like a sea in a storm and thundered its approval, my regrets returned manifold. Let me know when you are coming in, that I may secure tickets for you: the house is selling out now several days ahead, and we are turning hundreds of people away every night. Hooray!

I want very much to come out to Washington[1] for a day or two next week. . . . Be prepared to show me some nice hill-farms, which can be bought for a little money. I am looking for one.

Yours,

W. V. M.

In the spring of 1908, while living in rooms he had taken at 107 Waverly Place, New York, Moody was prostrated by a severe and prolonged attack of typhoid fever, from which his health never completely recovered. His hitherto stalwart constitution seemed broken and all work was hampered by a languor peculiarly hard for his active nature to endure. He was devotedly nursed by his friend of many years standing, Mrs. Harriet Brainerd, of Chicago, whom he married in 1909. The chief literary work of this time of broken health was the revision of "The Faith-Healer" for performance in January, 1910, and the drafting of the

[1] Washington, Connecticut.

WILLIAM VAUGHN MOODY

first act of "The Death of Eve," intended to complete
the trilogy of poetic dramas, but never finished. He
died October 17, 1910, at Colorado Springs.

To Henry Miller

HOTEL PONTCHARTRAIN.
DETROIT, Jan. 23rd, 1909.

MY DEAR MR. MILLER,

I saw the performance ["The Great Divide"]
this afternoon for the first time in many months,
and I am forced to protest against the way in
which the character of Philip has been gradually,
but at last in the end *totally*, changed, both in
spirit and significance. It is now played as a
comedy part, and the whole effort is spent upon
the attempt to wring the words and action, willy-
nilly, into the guise of comic relief. I need hardly
point out to you that this is to deprive the play
of an essential element and to very seriously
damage it thereby.

I make this statement with extreme unwilling-
ness, but I feel that I must do so both in fairness
to myself and in the interest of the play's future
integrity.

Believe me, Very sincerely yours,

WM. VAUGHN MOODY.

163

To Henry Miller

2970 GROVELAND AVE.
CHICAGO, Jan. 29, '09.

DEAR MR. MILLER,

I have not written before about the proposed change in the first act of the Great Divide, first because I have been again in bad health, but chiefly because I wanted to think it over from every point of view and see if it would "hold water" everywhere. I am now convinced, for my own part, that it is all right. The change is so slight and obvious a one that you will probably be skeptical at first of its efficacy, and in any case you will be surprised that it has not hitherto occurred to us. It is, in a word, simply to omit from the first act all mention of marriage. Ruth says merely "Save me, and I will make it up to you" (of course the dialogue here will have to be somewhat changed, but remains in substance the same, with the exception noted). She does not read the letter out, and its contents do not emerge until the second act. He speaks of reaching San Jacinto before daylight, but there is no mention of marriage there, although by this time and in the dialogue which follows it becomes clear (without any overt expression at all, and without any change) that marriage is in his mind. He reads (to himself) the note which she leaves for her brother, and it is here that the idea of marriage begins to take firm shape in his mind, but I do not think that the subject ought to be discussed or even broached between them. In the second act it is made clear that they *were* married on the very night of the attack, at San Jacinto, and the rest of the play goes on without change. What do you think? I have rewritten the first act on these lines, have criticised the result from every standpoint, and I firmly believe that the vexatious and long-standing problem is solved at last.

I have also made some verbal changes (chiefly omissions) in both the first and second acts, the reasons for which I will explain at length when I see you. I shall also tighten up the encounter between Ghent and Philip in Act III, so as to make of it a real menace on the brother's part.

I am unable to send you the revised manuscript at this moment, as I was forced by certain sudden complications in the matter of printing the book to send on the only copy I had to Houghton, Mifflin. This will be returned to me soon, when I shall forward it promptly to you. I have also been too ill to get in shape the detailed criticisms of the acting which I jotted down in Detroit, but as the company is to be practically re-made for England perhaps there is nothing to be gained by badgering the present actors with minute criticism. What do you think?

My doctor threatens, if I don't do better, to ship me off to Southern California. I hope this won't be necessary, or if necessary that I can get back in due season to watch the rehearsals of the Faith-Healer. Sincerely yours,

W. V. MOODY.

To Henry Miller

2970 GROVELAND AVE.
CHICAGO, Feb. 1st, '09.

DEAR MR. MILLER,

I have been doing very badly in health of late and am under doctor's orders to go to Southern California at once, on pain of a breakdown. This is very annoying to me, as I fear it will be also to you, but there is no getting round it. I have given orders to Houghton, Mifflin & Co., 4 Park St., Boston, to forward to your New York office promptly the proof-sheets of "The Great Divide," which will place before you my mature ideas concerning the changes already mentioned to you. Of course you are under no obligation to adopt them, but I hope that before rejecting any of them in favor of the old version you will give each change or omission your serious consideration. The slight (but I think important) changes in the second act are in the direction of softening the harsh asperity of Ruth's tone; also in one case (the omission of the lines: "Funny, ain't it — Well, I take my punishment" etc. "What are these papers?" "Plans for a sheep-corral ") to soften the harshness of Ghent's tone, which I think at this point grates on the nerves unduly. In the third act the only change of any importance is in the scene between Philip and Ghent, where I have tried to put some real menace into Philip's attack. If the stage directions are followed here, I feel sure the scene — and thereby the whole act — will be greatly strengthened.

Please, please persuade whoever plays Ruth in London to put love into Act II. Miss Lawton plays it without one hint of tenderness and smothered affection (or rather affection battling with pride), and in consequence her yielding to Ghent at the close of the play seems unconvincing — a mere theatrical forced note for the "happy ending," instead of seeming, as it really is, the final releasing of the flood-gates of her love. This is really, as you feel as strongly as I do, the master-note of the play. It has *never* been truly rendered, and at present it is not even *suggested*. This may sound like harsh criticism, but it is nevertheless gospel truth.

One thing more. I beg you to reconsider the stage business at the very close of Act I (I mean where Ghent raises his hand and points, and Ruth goes past him cringing with bent head). This seems to me melodramatic and false in its effect — it is quite out of key with Ghent's simple, straightforward, unmelodramatic character, and also with the girl's corresponding qualities. Please think of this. Also, I think the expression of Ghent's sorrow at the close of Act II is now over-done.

I think that his bursting into violent and audible grief alienates rather than wins the sympathy of the audience. You will forgive me for these frank criticisms. You asked me for them.

. . . .

I am sorry to inflict so long a letter upon you, but as my future is uncertain in the matter of health and whereabouts, I felt impelled to set these things down. Any word you can send me to my Los Angeles address, will be gratefully received;

I am anxious to keep in touch with your plans.
Sincerely yours,
WM. VAUGHN MOODY.

To Mrs. C. H. Toy

107 WAVERLY PLACE,
NEW YORK, Feb. 17 [1909.]

DEAR MRS. TOY,

. . . The new play ["The Faith-Healer"], of which you say you have heard, is a queerish thing, at the antipodes from this one ["The Great Divide"] in method and feeling. . . .

The thing I have most at heart just now is a poetic — I mean a *verse* — play. I have got a grand idea, and keep feeling my muscle to see if I am up to doing it, thus far with rather discouraging responses from my system. Also, I am torn between the ideal aspect of the theme and the stage necessities — the old, old problem. Perhaps in the end I will let the stage go to ballyhoo, and write the thing as I see it, for that justly lighted and managed stage of the mind, where there are no bad actors and where the peanut-eating of the public is reduced to a discreet minimum. But this — after all — is an uncourageous compromise. . . .

169

SOME LETTERS OF

[To Henry Miller]

Messrs. Brown, Shipley & Co.'s
Travellers' Office.
123, Pall Mall, London, S.W.
July 10, '09.

Dear Miller,

Your friendly telegram, letting me know the date of your arrival in London and inviting me to be present at the opening of the Divide, reached me yesterday. I have been meaning to write to you, to tell you how good the prospect looks to me here for the play, also to apologize to you for keeping mum at Sky Meadows this spring concerning my prospective marriage. The reason for my keeping quiet was — of course — my desire to prevent any inkling of the event from reaching the newspapers before we were safely on shipboard. Not that you would not have been discretion itself but one is always nervous in these matters. As it turned out, our precautions seem to have proved excessive, with the result that my mail swarms with inquiry from anxious friends. Cards of announcement after the fact are printed, and will I hope soon comfort these troubled breasts.

As to your invitation to be present at the open-

170

ing of the play, it greatly tempts me, and perhaps my desires will prevail over my prudence; but the fact is that my health has been and is wretched, and the doctors warn me that if I do not take great care just now I will rue it. The work which I did on the Faith-Healer, together with the excitement attending its production, came too soon after my typhoid convalescence. In consequence I broke down badly after reaching London, and have been extremely ill since, with symptoms of typhoid relapse well known to the doctors and very grimly regarded by them. Now I am better, and gaining steadily, but the wiseacres say that the only place for me — for a year — is a farm, and that any excitement which I allow myself is at my peril. Anyhow, I shall be here in spirit, and I cannot help feeling that the prospect for a substantial success is good, in fact excellent. . . .

With earnest good wishes, I am

Sincerely yours,

W. V. MOODY.

THE END